CENTENNIAL CELEBRATION.

PROCEEDINGS

IN CONNECTION WITH THE

Celebration at New Bedford,

SEPTEMBER 14th, 1864,

OF THE

TWO HUNDREDTH ANNIVERSARY

OF THE

INCORPORATION OF THE TOWN OF DARTMOUTH.

PRINTED BY ORDER OF THE CITY COUNCIL OF NEW BEDFORD.

New Bedford, Mass.
E. ANTHONY & SONS, PRINTERS, 67 UNION STREET.
1865.

At a meeting of the Committee of Arrangements, October 25th, 1864, James B. Congdon, the secretary, was requested to arrange for publication the addresses and other proceedings connected with the Centennial Celebration.

CONTENTS.

At a meeting of the City Council, October 6th, 1864, it was

Ordered, That five hundred copies of the proceedings on the occasion of the Centennial Celebration on the 14th day of September, 1864, and of the Addresses and Poem then delivered, be published under the direction of the committee of arrangements.

PROCEEDINGS

OF THE

CITY COUNCIL,

AND OF THE

COMMITTEE OF ARRANGEMENTS.

CENTENNIAL CELEBRATION.

MAYOR'S OFFICE,
CITY OF NEW BEDFORD,
2D MO. 11TH, 1864.

To the City Council:

GENTLEMEN, I herewith transmit to you an extract from the records of the Plymouth Colony, from which it appears that the town of Dartmouth, which included within its limits the territory embraced within our city, was established in June, 1664: and believing it might be satisfactory to many of our citizens, that some public notice should be taken of the return of the Second Centennial Anniversary of that event, permit me to suggest for your consideration the propriety of the adoption by the City Council of such measures for the commemmoration of that event, at some time during the coming summer, perhaps in the month of June, as in your judgment may be called for.

GEORGE HOWLAND, JUN., *Mayor.*

IN BOARD OF ALDERMEN,
February 11th, 1864.

Referred to a Joint Special Committee of two of which the Mayor shall be one, with such as the other branch may join.

HENRY T. LEONARD, *City Clerk.*

IN COMMON COUNCIL,
February 11th, 1864.

Concurred.

W. A. CHURCH, *Clerk.*

COMMITTEE.

His Honor, GEORGE HOWLAND, Jun., *Mayor.*
Alderman JOHN P. BARKER.
Councilmen, Messrs. CORNELIUS HOWLAND,
GEORGE F. KINGMAN, and
DANIEL HOMER.

By subsequent orders of the City Council the sum of one thousand dollars was placed at the disposal of the committee, and five hundred copies of the proceedings directed to be published.

EXTRACT

FROM THE

PLYMOUTH COLONY RECORDS.

COURT ORDERS.

1664
June 8

Att this Court, all that tracte of land called and known by the name of Acushena, Ponagansett and Coaksett is allowed by the Court to bee a townshipe: and the inhabitants thereof have libertie to make such orders as may conduce to theire good in towne consernments: and that the said towne bee hencforth called and knowne by the name of Dartmouth.

Fourth Book Court Orders, page 72.

The following notice was sent to the chairmen of the boards of selectmen of Dartmouth, Westport, Fairhaven, and Acushnet.

CITY OF NEW BEDFORD.

MAYOR'S OFFICE,
8th mo. 17th, 1864.

To ...., Chairman of the board of selectmen of..:

My friend, You are, with your colleagues of the board, respectfully requested to attend a meeting of the selectmen of Dartmouth, Westport, Fairhaven, and Acushnet, and of the committee of the city council of New Bedford, to be held at the mayor's office in the City Hall of said city, on the 19th instant, at 11 o'clock in the forenoon, for the purpose of making arrangements for the Centennial Celebration on the 7th of next month.

Respectfully,
GEORGE HOWLAND, JUN., Mayor.

The Trustees of the Free Public Library, having taken some action expressive of their interest in the proposed celebration, a committee of that body, consisting of its President the Mayor of the city, and Messrs. James B. Congdon and Henry J. Taylor, was requested to co-operate with the committee of the council in making the necessary arrangements.

MEETING OF COMMITTEE.

August 19th, 1864.

Present, His Honor the Mayor, and Messrs. Taylor, Kingman, and Congdon, of New Bedford.

From Dartmouth. Jireh Sherman and Calvin K. Turner, 2d, Esquires.

From Westport. Ezra P. Brownell, Esq.

From Fairhaven. Barth'w. Taber and Ellery T. Taber, Esquires.

From Acushnet. Hon. Cyrus E. Clark and Walter Spooner, Esq.

The mayor gave a welcome to the gentlemen from the neighboring towns, and informed them that the committee had fixed upon Wednesday, the 7th day of September next, for the celebration, and that William W. Crapo had consented to deliver an address and James B. Congdon a poem on the occasion. The object of the present meeting was to complete the arrangements.

The action of the city committee was approved by the meeting, after substituting the 14th, instead of the 7th, as the day for the celebration.

The meeting then proceeded to make all the necessary arrangements for the occasion.

Henry J. Taylor, Esq., was appointed Marshal of the day.

It was decided to have the exercises at the church of the First Christian Society, and a collation at the City Hall after the proceedings at the church should be over.

The following form of a notice was agreed upon and ordered to be published in the city papers.

CENTENNIAL CELEBRATION.

To the Sons and Daughters of Old Dartmouth abroad, the undersigned, on behalf of the children at home, send Greeting.

Two Hundred Years Ago

"The tracte of land called and known by the name of Acushnet, Ponagansett and Coaksett was allowed by the Court to bee a townshipe:—to bee henceforth called and knowne by the name of Dartmouth."

The villages which then formed the town of Dartmouth, now constitute the towns of Dartmouth, Westport, Fairhaven, and Acushnet, and the city of New Bedford.

On the 14th day of September next it is proposed to commemorate in New Bedford, by appropriate exercises, the completion of the second century since the incorporation of the parent town.

Our greeting is extended to all who, by birth, descent, marriage or former residence, may be supposed to feel an interest in the occasion.

To all such we cordially extend an invitation to unite with us in our *Family Re-union.*

We know that it will gladden *our* hearts, we trust it may *yours,* to meet as one household, upon the spot, consecrated by our fathers "two hundred years ago" to whatever "MIGHT CONDUCE TO THE GOOD OF THE INHABITANTS IN TOWN CONCERNMENTS."

GEORGE HOWLAND, JR.,
Mayor of New Bedford.
JIREH SHERMAN,
Chairman of Board of Selectmen of Dartmouth.
EZRA P. BROWNELL,
Chairman of Board of Selectmen of Westport.
BARTH'W TABER,
Chairman of Board of Selectmen of Fairhaven.
CYRUS E. CLARK,
Chairman of Board of Selectmen of Acushnet.

PROGRAMME.

The following programme was prepared by order of the committee of arrangements and published in the city papers.

CENTENNIAL CELEBRATION: September 14th, 1864.

The celebration of the Two Hundredth Anniversary of the incorporation of the ancient town of Dartmouth, will take place at New Bedford on Wednesday, the 14th day of September instant, under the direction of the several municipalities of Dartmouth, New Bedford, Westport, Fairhaven, and Acushnet.

There will be services at the Church of the First Christian Society; a Public Dinner at City Hall; and a Balloon Ascension from the Common.

EXERCISES AT THE CHURCH. The exercises at the Church will be an Address by His Honor GEORGE HOWLAND, Jr., Mayor of New Bedford.

An Address by WILLIAM W. CRAPO, Esq.,

A Poem by JAMES B. CONGDON, Esq.,

with appropriate Vocal and Instrumental Music.

DINNER AT CITY HALL. Plates will be laid in the hall for six hundred persons.

It is expected that His Excellency the Governor of the Commonwealth will be present with his military family. Other distinguished individuals, many of them from abroad, will attend as invited guests, from whom addresses appropriate to the occasion and the times may be expected.

Vocal and Instrumental Music will give diversity to the entertainment.

THE BALLOON ASCENSION. The Balloon Ascension will take place from the city common, at 5 o'clock, P. M.

The exercises at the Church will commence at 11 o'clock, A. M.

The invited guests, the selectmen of Dartmouth, Westport, Fairhaven, and Acushnet, the members of the New Bedford City Council, with the clerks of the two branches, and the town-clerks of the several towns, will assemble at the Mayor's room, in City Hall, at 10 o'clock.

At half after 10 they will proceed to the Church and occupy the seats reserved for them.

The Church will be opened at 10 o'clock for the admission of ladies, and gentlemen accompanied by ladies, to seats in any part of the building not reserved.

After the exercises at the Church the gentlemen occupying the reserved seats will return in a body to City Hall.

The ladies and gentlemen who hold tickets for the dinner, will assemble at the Council Chambers in the City Hall, at 1 o'clock. To avoid confusion the plates will be numbered to correspond with the number upon the tickets.

Tickets for the dinner may be obtained on and after the 8th instant, at the stores of Henry J. Taylor and Cornelius Davenport, where a plan of the tables may be seen.

Gentlemen holding cards of invitation have no occasion to provide tickets for the dinner.

I am requested by His Honor the Mayor, respectfully to desire the citizens of New Bedford to do all that may be in their power to render the occasion one of profit and enjoyment. His desire is that we may all close our places of business and open our hearts and our homes, that the celebration of the Two Hundredth Anniversary of the incorporation of our parent town may be long and pleasantly remembered.

HENRY J. TAYLOR, Marshal.

Cards of invitation were sent to a number of gentlemen resident abroad, and to some who are residents of New Bedford, requesting them to be present on the occasion as guests of the city. The following is a copy of a note sent to the Hon. Stephen Salisbury, President of the American Antiquarian Society.

CITY OF NEW BEDFORD,
September 5th, 1864.

To Hon. STEPHEN SALISBURY,
President of the American Antiquarian Society,
Worcester:

My friend. The two hundredth anniversary of the incorporation of the Old Town of Dartmouth, will be observed in New Bedford on the 14th instant by exercises appropriate to the occasion.

The gentlemen who act for the several municipalities

uniting in this celebration, are desirous that your society should be represented on the occasion.

Their invitation is hereby respectfully extended to you, and you may be assured that your presence will be a source of much gratification.

Should it not be in your power to attend in person, please confer a favor upon the committee by designating some other gentleman to honor us with his company and occupy the same position. I enclose a blank card of invitation, which please cause to be filled up as circumstances may require.

The favor of an answer is requested.

With much respect,

George Howland, Jr.,

Mayor of New Bedford.

A note of the same purport was sent to the Hon. Robert C. Winthrop, President of the Massachusetts Historical Society.

Letters from both these gentlemen will be found, with those from other invited guests in their appropriate place.

ORDER OF EXERCISES AT THE CHURCH.

1.

Music by the New Bedford Brass Band.

2.

Singing by the Choir.

Hymn:

Written for the occasion by James B. Congdon.

Eternal One! with solemn fear,
We speak thy high and holy name:
May every heart that name revere;
May every tongue Thy praise proclaim.

The Heaven of Heavens cannot contain
The Infinite! th' Unchangeable!
Nor can th' archangel's loftiest strain
The wonders of Thy glory tell.

Our God! our Father! Saviour! Friend!
Thy earthly children seek Thy face:
To all Thy gracious presence lend,
To all the blessings of Thy grace.

Thou wast our fathers' guide and stay,
Through years of peril and of blood:
Strong in Thy might they held their way,
And firm for God and Country stood.

They rest with Thee—their children here
In shade and storm their pathway tread:
Lord! in the cloud and flame appear,
And light and hope around us spread.

3.

Prayer:

By Rev. William J. Potter.

4.

Address:

By His Honor GEORGE HOWLAND, JR., Mayor of New Bedford.

5.

Singing by the Choir.

The Battle Hymn of the Republic:
Written by JULIA WARD HOWE.

Mine eyes have seen the glory of the coming of the Lord:
He is trampling out the vintage where the grapes of wrath are stored:
He has loosed the fatal lightning of His terrible swift sword.
His truth is marching on.
Glory! glory! hallelujah! Glory! glory! hallelujah!
Glory! glory! hallelujah! His truth is marching on.

I have seen Him in the watch-fires of a hundred circling camps;
They have builded Him an altar in the evening dews and damps:
I can read His righteous sentence by the dim and flaring lamps;
His day is marching on. Glory! &c.

I have read a fiery gospel writ in burnished rows of steel:
"As ye deal with my contemners, so with you my grace shall deal;"
"Let the hero born of woman crush the serpent with his heel;"
"Since God is marching on." Glory! &c.

He has sounded forth that trumpet which shall never call retreat;
He is sifting out the hearts of men before His judgment seat:
Be swift, my soul, to answer Him! be jubilant, my feet!
Our God is marching on. Glory! &c.

In the beauty of the lilies Christ was born across the sea,
With a glory in His bosom that transfigures you and me;
As he died to make men holy, let us die to make men free,
While God is marching on. Glory! &c.

6.

Address:

By William W. Crapo.

7.

Music by the Band.

8.

Poem:

By James B. Congdon.

9.

Music by the Band.

10.

Benediction:

By Rev. Tyler C. Moulton.

PROCEEDINGS

AT THE

CHURCH,

AND AT THE

CITY HALL.

On the day appointed for the celebration the arrangements made by the committee were fully carried into effect. The weather was delightfully pleasant. At 10 o'clock the invited guests assembled in the Aldermen's room, at the City Hall, where were also convened the members of the City Government; and at half past ten, a procession was formed by Henry J. Taylor, Esq., marshal of the day, which marched to the First Christian Church, on Purchase street, in the following order.

New Bedford Brass Band.
Marshal.
Common Council of New Bedford.
Clerk of the Common Council.
Board of Aldermen.
City Clerk.
Selectmen of Dartmouth, Westport, Fairhaven, and Acushnet.
Town Clerks.
Rhode Island and Massachusetts Christian Conference.
Invited Guests.
Mayor of New Bedford.
Orator, Poet, and Officiating Clergymen.

The proceedings at the church were in accordance with the order of exercises given above. The addresses by His Honor the Mayor and William W. Crapo, and the poem by James B. Congdon, will be found in their appropriate places in this publication. They were listened to by one of the largest and most respectable audiences ever collected in the city. The church was filled to its utmost capacity; and although the exercises occupied more than two hours, no evidence of weariness was exhibited on the part of the large gathering.

At the conclusion of the exercises at the church, the procession was re-formed and marched to the City Hall; and at two o'clock P. M. a large company of invited guests, and others from the city and the sister towns, sat down to a collation that had been provided.

Due attention having been given to the "creature comforts," Mayor Howland called the assembly to order. He expressed his pleasure at seeing so many present on the occasion, and invited their attention to the sentiments to be announced by the toast-master, and the responses which were expected.

C. B. H. Fessenden, Esq., who acted as toast-master, then announced the first sentiment.

"The President of the United States—honest and faithful Abraham Lincoln."

Hon. Thomas D. Eliot, representative from the first Congressional District, was called upon to respond to this sentiment, which he did in a most earnest and eloquent manner.

The second toast was,

"The Governor of Massachusetts—sound in head and heart; true to the State, careful of its interests, jealous for its honor, tender of its citizens, and true to the nation, the sovereign and safeguard of the State."

The Hon. Robert C. Pitman, state senator, made a beautiful and impressive response to this sentiment.

Mr. Fessenden then gave.

"The Army and Navy—more than sympathy, *all honor* to the brave and gallant soldiers and sailors, the true peace-makers, who, by their heroism in suffering and exploit, have added to the nation's glory, and through whose noble deeds we have assurance of the nation's safety."

Rev. William J. Potter, late chaplain in the United States army, spoke feelingly and forcibly of the deeds of the soldiers and sailors in the service of the country. In concluding his remarks he proposed the following sentiment.

"The free church, the free school, and the free ballot, we would defend and spread throughout the land, and open to all the inhabitants thereof."

The toast-master then read a letter from Hon. Robert C. Winthrop, President of the Massachusetts Historical Society, who had been invited, expressing his inability to be present, and requesting Ex-Governor Clifford to respond for the society of which he is a member.

The toast-master also, in this connection, alluded to the fact that in 1740, Dartmouth attempted something like a peaceable secession, and read the following extract from the ancient records of the town.

"Stephen West Jr. and Beriah Goddard are chosen agents in behalf of this town to apply to the honored court of Commissioners for the settling the line between Rhode Island and the Province of the Massachusetts Bay, and to show forth our desire and absolute right to come under the jurisdiction of the Colony of Rhode Island.

It was put to vote, whether it be the town's mind to come under the government of Rhode Island, *and it past by a very clear vote.*"

Fortunately, added Mr. Fessenden, this early attempt at secession failed to be consummated. But when he remembered that our distinguished townsman, who was called upon to respond for the Historical Society of Massachusetts, was a native of Rhode Island, had early in life removed to Old Dartmouth, and had served the Commonwealth of his adoption so acceptably, both as its chief Law Officer and as the head of its Government, he thought we might say, that although Dartmouth did not go to Rhode Island, the best part of Rhode Island came to Dartmouth—and gave as a sentiment:

"Our gain by this failure—one of Massachusetts' ablest Attorney Generals, and one of her purest Chief Magistrates."

To this sentiment Ex-Governor CLIFFORD was called upon by the Mayor to respond, and was received with cordial cheers.

He commenced by saying, that on behalf of the Massachusetts Historical Society, of which he believed he was the only member residing within the limits of the old town of Dartmouth, he desired to express his thanks to the committee for their courtesy in asking that the society might be represented upon this occasion. It was the oldest organization of the kind in this country—and the well-filled volumes of its collections and proceedings showed how diligent and efficient an association it had been in rescuing and preserving the valuable materials of history, which, but for its labors, would have been lost to the world. It had always regarded with great favor these local celebrations, furnishing as they do, such important and interesting contributions of those materials, and it had usually been represented at them by a committee of its members. If its accomplished President, whose letter had just been read, could have been present and listened to the exercises at the church this morning, he would have felicitated the society upon the valuable contributions to our local history which had been made both by the Orator and Poet of the day. The development by the former, in his admirable address, of the causes that led to the settlement of Dartmouth, elicited from the ancient records, hitherto so little known even to the students of our history, and demonstrating that our fathers were men who were ready to bear any burdens, or submit to any sufferings rather than sacrifice a great principle, could not have failed to impress him with a sense of the great value of these local investigations.

To the Poet also he would have felt, as the speaker did, a grateful sense of obligation for having added to the interesting episodes of our early history the verification of the fact that Major Andre, that most pathetic figure in the great drama of the Revolution, was an officer in Grey's Expedition, and witnessed from the spot on which we were assembled, the conflagration of Bedford village by the enemy.

The speaker also alluded to the justice that had been done by the Poet to that most conspicuous of all the Indian warriors with whom our Pilgrim Fathers had to contend for their existence as a colony—the son of the generous and magnanimous Massasoit, without whose faithful services and succor they must have perished—whom Washington Irving has so truthfully and beautifully described as "the brave and unfortunate King Philip; persecuted while living—slandered and dishonored when dead."

The speaker then proceeded to respond to the personal kindness which was conveyed in the sentiment offered by the Toast-master, and while expressing his grateful thanks for the favor with which it had been received by the company, remarked, that on an occasion like this, no one of the living could justly appropriate to himself, or have assigned to him by others any share in the honors of their festival. That in listening to the eloquent remarks of his friends, who had responded to the regular toasts from the chair, he could not forget, however worthy of our highest respect and most unreserved commendation were the subject of their eulogiums, that this was an occasion, not for the glorification of living Presidents, or Governors, or Generals, but one of commemoration of those who, by their services and sacrifices in their day and generation, had made Presidents and Governors and Generals possible in ours.

He then spoke at some length of the toils and sufferings of those by whom those sacrifices had been made, the fruits of which we were permitted to enjoy. He especially described in glowing terms the fidelity to every duty so conspicuously displayed by our Pilgrim Mothers, and the high-hearted women of the Revolution, whose resplendent virtue has reappeared among their descendants in this exigent hour of our country's agony; whose labors in behalf of the soldier in the field and the sailor on the deep, whose ministrations to the dying martyrs to their country's cause, in the hospitals and on the field of battle, proved that they had descended from a maternal ancestry, well worthy to be united with the fathers in this grateful service of commemoration.

Governor Clifford closed his address, of which the foregoing is only a meagre sketch, amid peals of applause, with the following sentiment.

"*The old town of Dartmouth*—Its founders were among the first to form a *union* to secure religious *liberty* for the individual: may their descendants be as steadfast and uncompromising in maintaining the '*Liberty* and Union, now and forever,' of their common country."

The next toast was,

"The Clergy—They owe much to those sturdy men of Old Dartmouth, who, though they refused to pay church rates, never failed to support honest and God-fearing ministers; and who, in a tolerant and catholic spirit, chose in 1730 as their religious teachers, Nicholas Howland, a Friend, and Philip Taber, a Baptist."

This called out the Rev. Doct. BABCOCK of Poughkeepsie, formerly of the William Street Baptist Church in this city, who pleasantly responded, and closed with the following:

"The absent sons of Old Dartmouth—Wherever they are, they remember their mother with undying affection."

Mr. Fessenden then read several of the many letters which had been received by the committee of arrangements in answer to invitations which had been sent to gentlemen who could not attend. These with others will be found at the conclusion of this account.

The following lines, written in response to the question, "What is there of interesting incident connected with the name of Dartmouth?" were read by the toast-master.

A Dartmouth* ship, to Dartmouth's shore†,
The bold adventurous Gosnold bore;
'T was Dartmouth's wide, historic strand*,
Sheltered the storm-tossed Pilgrim Band;
Against the wrong of British greed,
Hear * Dartmouth's Peer for justice plead;
A Dartmouth ship† with Dartmouth† crew,
With Dartmouth's† name and owner‡ too,
Had lading of th' historic tea,
Which found its steeping in the sea—
Wave-offering to Liberty.

In connection with this, JAMES B. CONGDON read an Address which he had prepared to the MAYOR, RECORDER

* Dartmouth in England. † Dartmouth in New England. ‡ The owner was Francis Rotch of Bedford in Dartmouth.

AND ALDERMEN OF THE CITY OF DARTMOUTH, COUNTY OF DEVON, ENGLAND.

The address was approved by the meeting; and a vote was passed, ordering its engrossment, and directing it to be sent, after being signed by the authorities of the several municipalities which united in making it, to those to whom it is addressed, by the committee of arrangements. The address and the vote of the assembly in relation to it will be found on a subsequent page.

Although ample provision had been made for prolonging the social and intellectual festivities of the occasion, five hours had now been devoted to them, and it was time for the parting song. This was admirably sung by several gentlemen, the whole company joining in the chorus.

Song:

Written for the occasion by WILLIAM G. BAKER, Esq.

No mournful strains to-day we sing,
  No requiem for the Past,
As here, fresh laurel wreaths we bring,
  On victor's heads to cast.
Though twice one hundred years are o'er,
  They live who lived so well,
And by Acushnet's peaceful shore
  In honor yet they dwell.
      Then let the swelling chorus ring
      For days of "auld lang syne."
      Till echoes answer, as we sing
      The brave of "auld lang syne."

The tranquil river onward flows,
  And still rolls in the sea,
While autumn's sun serenely glows
  On laden vine and tree.
But where are they whose names we love,
  Whose treasured deeds we boast?

Not where the crumbling stones above,
  Record them with the lost.
      Then let the swelling chorus ring, &c.

They live in every glorious word
  Defending freedom's cause,
They strike, where falls the patriot's sword
  For Union and the laws.
And when the brave host marching goes
  To battle for the right,
Their footsteps mark the spot, where foes
  Fall thickest in the fight.
      Then let the swelling chorus ring, &c.

The vine shall in the dust decay,
  And withered fall the tree;
Old Time shall hew these shores away,
  And trample down the sea:
But Fame shall keep their record bright,
  Who builded for us here,
As long as right shall still be right
  And liberty be dear.
      Then let the swelling chorus ring
      For days of "auld lang syne,"
      Till echoes answer, as we sing
      The brave of "auld lang syne."

Thus was brought to a close the celebration of the two hundredth anniversary of the incorporation of the town of Dartmouth. It was an interesting and delightful occasion. Of the large number of the people of this city and the sister communities who participated in it, not one appeared to be disappointed. It was a day of elevated enjoyment and profitable recreation; and that a record of it may be preserved and a portion of the pleasure it imparted may be participated in by those who were not present, this account of its proceedings has been prepared and published.

It belongs to the history of our Centennial to state, that the music both at the church and at the hall was of an unusually high character. Mrs. Howe's "Battle Hymn of the Republic" was sung in a manner that gave it access to the breasts of the immense audience, which was fully evidenced by the heartiness with which they joined in the magnificent chorus. To Mr. Barton Ricketson, Jr., who kindly volunteered to take charge of the singing, the public are greatly indebted for the effective manner in which this part of the exercises was performed. It is hardly necessary to say that the New Bedford Brass Band performed, in an admirable manner, the patriotic airs they had selected for the occasion.

The record would be incomplete, did it fail to notice the promptness and good order with which the arrangements were carried into effect by the marshal of the day, Henry J. Taylor, Esq., and his efficient corps of assistants, Messrs. Andrew G. Pierce, Lemuel M. Kollock, Cornelius Davenport, John W. Macomber, William C. Taber, Jr., and Charles H. Gifford.

THE PHOTOGRAPHS

OF THE

EARLY DARTMOUTH RECORDS.

James B. Congdon, who has been for a long time at work upon the official records of Dartmouth, arranging the scattering fragments, and restoring many imperfect and fast decaying pages, exhibited photographs of the two oldest existing pages of these records. They are the work of the Brothers Bierstadt, and convey a perfect idea of the ancient, dim and defaced originals. Copies are, we understand, to be presented to each of the municipalities whose connection with the old records renders these pictures of the first recorded proceedings of the town interesting and valuable. It is understood that Mr. Congdon will continue his labors upon these records until they are as nearly restored as their dilapidated condition will admit.

The following is a transcript of the first page of the records of which a photograph copy has been taken as before stated.

"At a town meeting the 22: of May in the year: 1674. John Cook was chosen debity arther hathaway grandiuryman William earl Constable John Russell iams Shaw and William Palmer selectmen daniel willcoks peleg Shearman and Samuel Cudbard survaers and James Shaw Clark.

At a town meetinge ye 22 of Jouly 1674 it is ordered that all our town meetings doe beginne at ten of ye clocke and to continue untill ye moderator doly releace the town not exceeding four of ye clocke.

It is all so ordered that all such parsons as doe necklectt to a yeer all the town meetings shall for fitt to the town 1 shilling and six pence a pece and for coming to meeting to leatt three pence an hour.

It is all so ordered that the town clarke shall gather up all a for said finnes and shall have y^e on hallfe of them for his pains and in ceace any doe refuse to pay them returne the neame to ye towne.

It is ordered by the towne by vote that there shall be no alteration in the rulle of............ for this following year.

Henry Tucker Joseph Tripp and Jeames Shaw are chosen reatters for this following yeer.

At a town meeting in the 17 of May 1675 John Cook is chosen deputy for this following year. John Russell is chosen constable for this following year. Joseph Allinne is chosen Grandiuryman for this following year William Earlle Acha Howland Junior Thomas briggs are suruires for this following year.

Whereas there is complaint .... of the badness of .... fences the town hereby chosen thomas teabor and Jeames Shaw for Acushenett and John Smith and pelige Shearman for ponegansett and pelige tripp and William Wood for acocksett to vew mens fences and .... to .... them for a .... fence or condemn and to fine .... and bad to mend them."

ADDRESS

TO THE PEOPLE OF

DARTMOUTH, ENGLAND.

ADDRESS.

To the Mayor, Recorder and Aldermen of the City of Dartmouth, County of Devon, England:

GENTLEMEN, On this day of our solemn festivity, while we are assembled to commemorate the incorporation, two hundred years ago, of the town called by a name which your historic city has borne for nearly a thousand, we, the people of the city of New Bedford, and of the towns of Dartmouth, Westport, Fairhaven and Acushnet, municipalities into which the territory of the mother town has been separated, would to you, and through you to the inhabitants you represent, send a greeting of remembrance and regard.

Forcibly and pleasantly have we at this time been reminded of the many interesting circumstances which connect your ancient borough with the town whose corporate birth-day we now commemorate. We call to mind the fact, that it was from Dartmouth, and in a Dartmouth ship, bearing a name significant of that feeling of CONCORD which will we trust forever characterize the intercourse between the nations to which we respectively belong, that BARTHOLOMEW GOSNOLD in 1602 put forth upon his voyage to America, landed upon *our* shores, and upon an island often called by his name, in sight from the spot upon which we are now assembled, erected the first white man's dwelling upon the soil of NEW ENGLAND.

Deeper still have been our recollective associations as we have remembered, that it was in your noble harbor, and in the nobler hearts and homes of the then inhabitants of your city, that our Pilgrim Fathers found a shelter, when the perils of the storm drove them from their course across the ocean to found an empire in the NEW WORLD. It was the memory of that providential preservation, and of the hospitality extended to them in that hour of despondency and weakness, that prompted them, when they went forth from Plymouth Rock to subdue the forest and extend the borders of their Commonwealth, to bestow upon this portion of their goodly heritage the name of that city by the Mouth of the Dart, from which they had taken their last departure for their new home amid the wilds of America.

The occasion demanded of those who had been selected to address us a brief recital of that conflict which led to the political separation of the United States of America from the land our people have ever loved to call the MOTHER COUNTRY.

And while we have been moved and saddened by the recital, we have with deep and grateful feelings remembered, that it was WILLIAM LEGGE, Earl of Dartmouth, Secretary of the Colonies under George 3d, and who derived his title from your ancient city, who gave the force of his character and commanding talents in opposition to the Grenville Administration, for conciliation and peace. For the memory of this friend of Franklin, the friend of justice, the friend of peace, this high-minded Christian gentleman and Peer of England, we shall ever cherish the sentiments of profound respect.

Such are some of the links of that Golden Chain of associations which at this moment stretches across the ocean, and binds together the city whose noble harbor sheltered the crusading fleet of the LION-HEARTED RICHARD, with the family of communities which are resting near the waters of GOSNOLD'S HOPE. We would add, as a circumstance calculated to strengthen the force of the historic reminiscences to which we have alluded, that we, too, are to a great extent a family of fishermen. At a period not remote, a whaling fleet of nearly four hundred ships belonging to the communities we represent, manned by more than ten thousand seamen, was afloat upon the ocean.

We would assure you, gentlemen, that in sending you this

greeting, which finds its justification in, and depends for its interest upon, the incidents and circumstances we have recited, we have a purpose deeper than the extension of a compliment, or the indulgence of pleasant and interesting associations. We wish not to withhold the expression of the fact, that in the civil strife which is now raging in our land, its loyal people would fain have extended to them that moral encouragement and support that attends upon the favorable testimony of enlightened Englishmen. They feel that they are doing battle for principles which they have derived from their Saxon ancestry, and dear to the heart of every Briton.

Allow us, therefore, to express the hope, that the reception of our earnest and affectionate greeting will give such a direction to your feelings and lead to such an examination of the questions at issue between us and our infatuated Southern fellow-countrymen, as shall result in your giving the weight of your enlightened minds and the testimony of your Christian character to the cause of universal freedom. We address you amidst the smoke and the roar of the conflict; but we hope and believe that the end is near—and when peace shall be restored and the flag of our country shall again wave over an undivided soil and a united people, we feel assured that such will then be our condition, that closer than it has ever been before will be the union between us and our MOTHER COUNTRY.

New Bedford, Sept. 14, 1864.

The following is a copy of the vote passed in connection with the foregoing address, by the company at the City Hall.

Voted, That the address to the Corporate Authorities and the people of the ancient city of Dartmouth, in the county of Devon, in England, which has now been read, be adopted—that it be properly engrossed*—that it be signed

* The copy of this address which is to be sent across the Atlantic, has been prepared by George B. Hathaway of this city. It is a beautiful piece of work, and will add to the high reputation which Mr. Hathaway has long sustained for excellence as a chirographer.

on behalf of the people of Dartmouth, New Bedford, Westport, Fairhaven and Acushnet by their respective corporate authorities, and authenticated by the seals of the several municipalities—and that, when thus prepared, it be forwarded to those for whom it is intended by the committee of arrangements, in such a manner as they shall think proper.

LETTERS

FROM

INVITED GUESTS.

LETTERS declining the invitations of the committee of arrangements were received from His Excellency Governor Andrew, Hon. Henry H. Crapo of Michigan, Rev. Orville Dewey, Hon. Alexander H. Bullock, Hon. J. H. W. Page, Martin L. Eldridge, Esq., Thomas Almy, Esq., Hon. Robert C. Winthrop, President Massachusetts Historical Society, Rev. Charles Ray Palmer, Hon. Lemuel Williams, Rev. W. S. Studley, Daniel Ricketson, Esq., Hon. Stephen Salisbury, President of the American Antiquarian Society, and others.

Want of space restricts the publication to the communications received from the gentlemen whose names we have given.

From His Excellency John A. Andrew.

BOSTON, September 10, 1864.

Hon. GEORGE HOWLAND, Jr.,
Mayor, &c., New Bedford, Mass:

MY DEAR SIR, I sincerely regret that a visit to Washington, which is important to be made immediately, will prevent my enjoying the pleasure I had anticipated in attending the centennial celebration at New Bedford on the 14th instant. The occasion is one of intrinsic interest; and I am sure that the gentlemen who will assist in its illustration will not fail to render it an honorable and pleasant memorial of your beautiful and prosperous city. I trust that I may be able partially to compensate myself for the loss I shall suffer, both of instruction and recreation, in being obliged to decline your friendly and valued invitation, not only by reading the addresses and proceedings which will be doubtless in print hereafter, but also by finding some other early opportunity of enjoying your hospitality.

I am, with much regard, your friend and servant.

JOHN A. ANDREW.

From Hon. Henry H. Crapo.

FLINT, Mich., August 29, 1864.

Hon. GEORGE HOWLAND, Jr.,
Mayor of the City of New Bedford, Mass.:

MY DEAR SIR, I am in receipt of your esteemed favor of the 24th inst., inclosing the invitation of yourself and the several chairmen of the Boards of Selectmen for the towns of Dartmouth, Westport, Fairhaven and Acushnet, to be present, on the 14th proximo, at the "celebration of the two hundredth anniversary of the incorporation of the town of Dartmouth."

I am indeed gratified, not only by the invitation itself, but more especially by *your* friendly and flattering letter inclosing it; and be assured that nothing short of an imperious necessity would deprive me of the exquisite pleasure I should most certainly enjoy by being present on that occasion, and taking by the hand my old and well remembered friends, and exchanging once more with them those cordial and heartfelt greetings so expressive of mutual friendship and regard.

But I regret to say, that notwithstanding my most earnest desire to be present, circumstances are such that I am compelled to deny myself the pleasure.

The occasion will undoubtedly be a source of great enjoyment to all who are permitted to be present; whilst to those who are not it will be a prolific source of reflection, consequent upon a review of the past, and of the various changes incident to human life, which the occasion can hardly fail to call up.

In regard to myself, as I peruse your kind and friendly letter, my mind is at once forcibly and irresistibly carried back through all the varied scenes and amid all the numerous associations of a period of nearly *fifty* years of vivid recollection; and as these pass in review before me, I again behold, at least in imagination, the spot where I was born in that, even *now*, apparently new and unclaimed and uncultivated region in the north part of the present town of Dartmouth—and further on, in another portion of her territory, I see the old and worn out fields, with their hard, sterile and rocky soil, in which my boyhood and youth were spent in a round of unceasing toil;—whilst in the foreground of the picture appears in vivid colors all the scenes and incidents and associations consequent upon a busy life, in the prime of manhood—surrounded by warm and true and devoted friends—for a period of nearly *thirty* years in your own beautiful city.

How forcibly your invitation and your kind letter recall to my mind all the important events of my whole life, until Providence, by some mysterious influence, directed my steps to Michigan, the State of my adoption—my present home—and where I trust my future days will be spent.

But although now an acknowledged citizen of Michigan, a State still in its infancy, yet destined ere long to stand at the head of the States of this Union in prosperity, in wealth, and in refinement, as well as in every material element of greatness and power—whose area is nearly as large as that of all New England, and whose population in the brief space of a few years has nearly reached that of the good old State of Massachusetts—whose soil is rich and productive—whose climate is healthy—whose society is good—and whose people are intelligent, enterprising and industrious—and whose resources, the development of which has scarcely begun, in almost every variety of the richest and most useful mineral substances, as well as in vast forests of choice timber, and in extensive fisheries—are of incalculable value;—and although in some at least of these particulars the comparison may be to the disadvantage of our native town, whose birth you commemorate, yet after all, for one of her sons, I must bear unqualified testimony that what she may lack in some things she amply makes up in others. And although I am well pleased with and proud of the home of my adoption, yet I still appreciate and love, and will ever strive to honor, as she deserves, my native home.

And to her sons and daughters who may meet with you on this occasion I would say, that I am proud of "Old Dartmouth," the place of my birth, and the home of my childhood, my youth, and my manhood for so many years; and that the recollection of all her dealings towards me, one of her truant sons, are ever sweet and grateful, for they were infinitely above my deserts.

Let me also say to those who still abide by the old "roof-tree," and who still cling to "Fader Land," and let me ask those who like me have strayed from the fold, to unite in the sentiment, that it shall ever be our study, our constant and unalterable purpose, wherever we may be in the future, in whatever position the calls of duty may place us, or under whatever circumstances our lives may be cast, that we will remain true to our native land, that we will foster and cherish every right principle of our fathers, that we will hold fast to the lessons, and constantly maintain the habits of industry, prudence, and virtue, which we received upon her rugged soil, and that we will ever honor that dear old home, which has given us, by her efficient training, a will to overcome difficulties and to surmount obstacles, and an ambition for right progress and for honorable advancement, that is not excelled by the sons of any other soil.

If we do this, I am sure that whether still denizens of the "Dear Old Home," or wanderers in more highly favored lands, we shall have no just cause to regret, but shall remember with an honest pride, that the "Old Dartmouth" of 1664 was the place of our birth; nor will that home have occasion to regret that we are her sons, or blush to acknowledge us as her children.

You have my dear sir, been pleased to allude, in very friendly and flattering terms, to the circumstance, that my son is the chosen orator of the day. I am indeed proud to learn that he is deemed worthy, on such an occasion, of occupying so prominent a position; and I may perhaps be pardoned this expression of my gratification.

With sentiments of the highest esteem and regard to

yourself personally, and to your associates, and with the most friendly and cordial greetings to all who may be present on the occasion,

I remain, very truly, yours, &c.

HENRY H. CRAPO.

From Rev. Orville Dewey.

SHEFFIELD, Sept. 8th, 1864.

To the Mayor of New Bedford, and his Associates:

GENTLEMEN, I have received your invitation to the coming two hundredth anniversary. Circumstances make it inconvenient for me to take the journey at the present time; but I thank you for remembering me on this occasion, and thus recognizing my claim to belong to New Bedford. I belong to it, though not by birth, yet by a residence there, during the first ten years of my professional life. Thirty years have passed since; and time, I must suppose, has weakened any interest felt in me, more than it has mine, in the good old town—so many of whose dwellings and very streets are dear to my recollection.

Thirty years is the life-time of a generation; and more than six of those periods have passed since the first settlements were made at Buzzard's Bay. Six generations, now swelling, I suppose, to 30 or 40,000 people—what worlds, if earnest and anxious, of sad and joyous life, since the first settlers came! Pleasant place they came to; I do not wonder that they were attracted to them—the banks of the Acushnet; the view-commanding slopes of New Bedford; the lovely Point, skirted now, by a magnificent Promenade Road; and the quiet fields and shores of Padanaram—pleasant to my remembrance, like the scenes of the old Bible story—like "the memory of joys that are past, pleasing and mournful to the soul."

The commemoration of epochs is the recognition of a history. And New Bedford has a history; in its arduous and prosperous business; in its growing wealth; in its public schools; in its flourishing Lyceum,* and in its goodly tabernacles of worship; in the strong moral tone, and, as I well believe, in these perilous times, the Devoted Loyalty of its people.

I send to it, on its honored two hundredth anniversary, my respectful and affectionate greeting.

ORVILLE DEWEY.

From Hon. Alexander H. Bullock.

WORCESTER, Sept. 4, 1864.

MY DEAR SIR, I thank you for the invitation to attend the two hundredth anniversary of the incorporation of Dartmouth, and only regret that my engagements on the 14th instant will prevent my attendance.

There is peculiar signification in these municipal celebrations at a time like the present. Massachusetts owes what she is and what she has accomplished, to her municipal individualities. Their culture, their patience and trials, their patriotism and sacrifices, have made up her sovereign power, and crowned her with glory. In them she learned Liberty. From them she derived those lessons of government, of economy, of virtue, which she has promulgated over this country and over the globe. These are the nurseries of her principles, her faith, her all.

Looking back over a period of two centuries, how the inhabitants of the ancient town, now become five, may congratulate themselves that the great principles of Liberty and Government, now in the peril of war, have at all times and under all difficulties, had a shrine there! I believe, also, that after such a survey and review, your fellow-citizens will arouse with fresh stimulation to the manly defence of those blessings which their ancestors achieved by their toil,

* Doct. Dewey wrote the notice for publication that called the first meeting in relation to the Lyceum.

their treasure, and their blood, and which are now placed in hazard by an atrocious rebellion.

May the lesson of Liberty be treasured and transmitted!

Yours most truly,

ALEXANDER H. BULLOCK.

His Honor GEORGE HOWLAND, Jr., and others.

From Hon. J. H. W. Page.

BOSTON, Sept. 3d, 1864.

To the Mayor of New Bedford, and his Associates:

MY DEAR SIR, I have received yours, enclosing invitation to attend the "two hundredth anniversary of the incorporation of the town of Dartmouth," on Wednesday, Sept. 14.

I need not tell you how much my heart is interested in that matter. I *love* New Bedford, although fate has for some years placed me elsewhere. If I can ever do her good, I shall do it with all my heart.

I expect to leave for Pennsylvania Monday morning, and shall not probably return before the 14th. If I should, I will be with you.

If I am not there, please take my kindest sympathies and best wishes with you all.

Ever gratefully and truly yours,

J. H. W. PAGE.

From Martin L. Eldridge, Esq., of Acushnet, Teacher in the State Nautical School.

DEAR SIRS, Your kind invitation to be present at "the two hundredth anniversary of the incorporation of the town of Dartmouth," was duly received. I fear my engagements are such as to deprive me of the happiness of being with you on that interesting occasion.

Dartmouth, in point of time the twelfth town in the Colony of Plymouth, was settled in a dark and stormy period. In England, the transient joy of an afflicted people at the restoration of a Stuart king was giving way under the encroachments of new tyrannies, to well-grounded fears and gloomy discontent. The unsettled policy of the parent country towards its infant colonies was now assuming a shape which filled the colonists with the greatest apprehensions and misgiving. A fleet of ships of war was crossing the Atlantic, bearing an obnoxious commission and armed soldiery to the shores of New England; and the deepest solicitude was felt for the fate of the colonies.

Bnt the determined men of those days turn not from their settled purpose. They erect new townships, they subdue the wilderness, and, unmindful of hardships, perils, or discouragements, build as for a bright future.

What a sublime example of faith in God and a good cause!

Let us hope that the lessons taught by the retrospect of two centuries may increase our veneration for those remarkable men who laid the political foundations, not of a municipality merely, but of the Republic; who amid perils *we* can never justly estimate, with unexampled fortitude, battled in those early days for human freedom.

Let it not be forgotten that it was from the Colony of Plymouth that the first suggestion of UNION came; and in coming time, whatever communities of men may forsake the faith and doctrines of her Fathers, on the soil of the Old Colony let us hope a people may be found whose devotion to "Liberty and Union" shall be forever unconquered and unconquerable.

Very truly yours,

MARTIN L. ELDRIDGE.

To GEORGE HOWLAND, Jr., and others.

From Thomas Almy, Esq.

"QUANSETT," Sept. 13th, 1864.

DEAR SIRS, I am very grateful, as one of the inhabitants of the ancient town of Dartmouth, for the generous hospitality tendered us by the citizens of New Bedford.

Having nearly reached my ninetieth year, I fear that the undertaking and excitement would be too much for me; otherwise it would afford me great pleasure to be present at so agreeable a re-union.

I trust that this festival will be the means of strengthening the bonds of sympathy and good-fellowship for future generations.

I am, very truly, yours,

THOMAS ALMY.

[A. B. ALMY, Scribe.]

Messrs. GEORGE HOWLAND, Jr., Mayor, and others.

From Hon. Robert C. Winthrop, President Massachusetts Historical Society.

BOSTON, 10th Sept. 1864.

Hon. GEORGE HOWLAND, Jr.,

Mayor of New Bedford:

MY DEAR SIR, I have the honor to acknowledge your obliging communication, inviting me to represent the Massachusetts Historical Society at the "Old Dartmouth" festival on the 14th instant.

I regret extremely that previous engagements for that day will prevent my being with you. It would have given me great pleasure to unite in commemorating the two hundredth anniversary of the incorporation of a town, which, in addition to its own bright record of usefulness and honor, is able to exhibit, as one of its numerous offspring, the noble city over which you are privileged to preside.

I offer you the congratulations of the Massachusetts Historical Society on the occasion of so memorable an anniversary. It carries us back to a period when that old Mother Country, of which Plymouth and Massachusetts were but humble colonies, was rejoicing in the restoration of peace and prosperity after a long and bloody civil war. Let us hope that our own day of Restoration is not far distant; and that Peace and Union and Constitutional Liberty may soon be welcomed again throughout the length and breadth of our beloved land.

I will endeavor, agreeably to your request, to make arrangements for the representation of our Society at your festival by some other one of our officers or members. But if no other should appear, your valued fellow-citizen, Governor Clifford, is one of our number, and we should gladly leave it to him to speak for us on an occasion in which he cannot but feel the deepest interest.

I am, respectfully and truly,

Your obliged and obedient servant,

ROBERT C. WINTHROP.

From Rev. Charles Ray Palmer.

SALEM, 12th Sept. 1864.

[After mentioning that illness would prevent him from being present at the festival, Mr. Palmer says:]

I have a great interest in Old Dartmouth, and a high appreciation of the usefulness, from many points of view, of such a celebration as is proposed. It will quicken those local attachments which seem to be part of, if not essential to, true patriotism. It will have a great value to the historiographer. It will collect and secure the permanent preservation of much traditional information, that soon would be forgotten. It will also be an interesting occasion for the interchanging and the cultivation of those friendly affections that refine and adorn our social life.

My interest in Old Dartmouth is owing to the connection with its early history of William Palmer, from whom I am a descendant of the seventh generation. He was born in Plymouth, June 27th, 1664. His father and grandfather, (both "Williams,") were among the "Old Comers," having landed in the Fortune at Plymouth, Nov. 9, 1621. William Palmer, Jr., was, at the date of his landing, about eight years old. He died in Plymouth in 1635 or 1636, leaving a wife and two children. William of Dartmouth, his son, married first a daughter of Robert Paddock, of Plymouth, who soon died; second, Susannah Hathaway, who survived him. He died in 1679, having been constable, surveyor, and selectman. He received other marks of the respect of his fellow-citizens. His older sons (two) removed to Little Compton in 1684. The remainder of his family continued in Dartmouth. Mrs. Philip Dunham (Ruth Palmer) of Dartmouth, is a descendant of the fifth generation. The late Richard A. Palmer, of New Bedford, was of the sixth.

Very respectfully yours,

CHARLES RAY PALMER.

His Honor GEORGE HOWLAND, Jr., and others, committee.

From Hon. Lemuel Williams.

WORCESTER, Sept. 12th, 1864.

GENTLEMEN, I received your invitation to attend the Centennial Celebration of the two hundredth anniversary of the incorporation of the town of Dartmouth, and should have gladly complied with it, if my health would have permitted.

Not being able to attend in person, I commenced a sketch of my knowledge of many interesting incidents in the history of that ancient town, my reminiscences of what have been told me by my father and other aged persons, extending back more than one hundred and fifty years, but ill health has prevented my completing it, which I regret, as many of these incidents remain only in my recollection.

With many thanks for your kind invitation,

I am respectfully, your obedient servant,

LEMUEL WILLIAMS.

Messrs. GEORGE HOWLAND, Jr., and others,
Committee of two hundredth anniversary.

From Rev. W. S. Studley.

BOSTON, Sept. 12, 1864.

DEAR SIRS, I thank you heartily for your invitation to the Dartmouth "Centennial." As a former resident of New Bedford—one of her territorial progeny—it would afford me real pleasure to be present with my adopted grandmother's household to celebrate her two hundredth birthday; but my other duties, I fear, will prevent. Through you, I herewith extend to the whole family my best wishes for a happy re-union. I have little skill at "sentiment," but here is one honest wish.

Dartmouth, the aged matron—mother of cities—in time to come, as now, may her children be her proudest jewels.

Yours, truly,

W. S. STUDLEY.

Messrs. GEORGE HOWLAND, Jr., and others.

From Daniel Ricketson, Esq.

BROOKLAWN, 10th Sept. 1864.

FRIENDS AND FELLOW-CITIZENS, While I yield to my disinclination to be present at public festivities, I can most heartily unite with you in the commemoration of the first settlement of the old township of Dartmouth, within whose limits stands our beloved city.

As a native of New Bedford, and in a line of six generations from the first settler of my family name, who was also one of the original proprietors of the township in the "eight-hundred-acre division," I need not assure you how much I am interested in the welfare and success of the several members of the ancient township, comprising the present towns of Dartmouth, Westport, New Bedford, Fairhaven, and Acushnet.

The early settlers of Dartmouth, as is known to many of you, were mostly Friends, and to their industry, as well as to their moral and religious character, we owe much of the prosperity of our place; not only in the cultivation of the soil, whereby they left a goodly heritage to their posterity, but in the more venturesome employment upon the ocean.

"The father of the whale fishery," as he has sometimes been called, though not himself a sailor, was Joseph Russell, a Friend, whose house stood within the memory of many of us, on County street, near the head of William.

He was an extensive land-holder whose domain comprised several hundred acres, now in the most busy and prosperous part of our city. His cart-way to the shore was on Union street, known prior to the Revolution as King street, and then as the Main street of our boyhood.

It was not however, until the removal from Nantucket of those eminent merchants, William Rotch, Sen'r, and William Rotch, Jr., and Samuel Rodman, Sen'r, that New Bedford became known much abroad as a commercial place. Others of our own people soon became engaged in business, and before the last war with the Mother Country, our place had become known to most of the commercial emporiums of Europe, whither our vessels had carried cargoes of oil, bringing return cargoes of the products of other lands, many of them articles of manufacture for household and agricultural use.

Although I have not personally taken a prominent part in the affairs of our city, none the less have I felt interested in her welfare; and while much is to be said in her praise, a word of counsel and caution may not be out of place. The looker-on at a play may oftentimes better see and understand it than they who take parts therein: so often while observing the state of our affairs in the several fields of public interest, whether civil, commercial or religious, I have regretted the apparent decay of that ancient good faith and integrity which so marked the founders of our city, and in lieu thereof, that struggle for wealth irrespective of the rights of others.

The society of New Bedford from thirty to fifty years ago, would by no means lose in the comparison with that of the present. It could show many highly cultivated minds, of both sexes, and few houses of the better class but had their library, though small, of the choicest literature of the English language, while a generous and hospitable spirit almost universally prevailed.

Better days are, I trust, still in store for us, when the fierce spirit of war shall be quelled and the smiling spirit of peace shall return once more to our bleeding and sorrow-stricken people, which will undoubtedly be best secured by a close attention to those higher and more sacred interests of our moral and religious natures.

Thanking you for your kind invitation, and with my best wishes for the success of the celebration,

I remain your friend and fellow-citizen,

DANIEL RICKETSON.

Hon. GEORGE HOWLAND, Jr., Mayor,
and the other members of the committee.

From Hon. Stephen Salisbury, President of the American Antiquarian Society.

HALL OF THE AMERICAN ANTIQUARIAN SOCIETY,
Worcester, Sept. 13, 1864.

Hon. GEORGE HOWLAND, Jr.,
Mayor of the city of New Bedford:

MY DEAR SIR, Returning home yesterday afternoon from an excursion of a week, I find your respected letter of 5th instant, which invites the American Antiquarian Society to the honor and satisfaction of participating in the celebration of the two hundredth anniversary of the incorporation of the good old town of Dartmouth, which will take place to-morrow. I present the thanks of the American Antiquarian Society for this distinguished hospitality, and I thank you for the personal compliment of the request, that I should represent the Society.

As I have an official engagement that must detain me from the enjoyment which you offer, I have attempted to exercise the privilege you offer to me, in selecting some other member to go as a delegate of our society, and at so short notice I have not been successful, to my great regret.

This society has the deepest interest in the combined efforts of the prosperous dwellers within the limits of that venerable town, to honor the virtues of the Fathers and to open the sources of history, which may show whence the life-blood and strength of that wealthy and intelligent population was derived.

Will you permit me to offer the sentiment written below and to assure you

Of my high and grateful respect?

STEPHEN SALISBURY,

President American Antiquarian Society.

"Old Dartmouth, the comely mother of more beautiful children, whose prosperity has a diverse origin. 'The depth says it is wholly in me,' for their line has gone out through all the earth, and their enterprise encompasseth the land and the sea."

ADDRESS

OF

HIS HONOR GEORGE HOWLAND, JR.,

MAYOR OF NEW BEDFORD.

ADDRESS.

My friends and fellow-citizens of Old Dartmouth:

LADIES AND GENTLEMEN, We are convened this day on an occasion of no ordinary interest. We are met to commemorate the two hundredth anniversary of the incorporation of the town of Dartmouth in the year 1664. We find in the records of the Plymouth Colony for the year the following:

"1664, June.—Att this Court, all that tracte of land comonly called and knowne by the name of Acushena, Ponagansett and Coaksett, is allowed by the Court to bee a townshipe, and the inhabitants thereof have libertie to make such orders as may conduce to theire comon good in town consernments; and that the said towne bee henceforth called and knowne by the name of Dartmouth."

The territory within the limits described in that record, includes the present towns of Dartmouth, Westport, Fairhaven, and Acushnet, and the city of New Bedford, and was at that time probably an almost unbroken wilderness; how different now! Where to-day we find the bustle and din of business, hear the hum of the spindle and the shriek of the locomotive, and see the gallant ships entering our harbors freighted with the rich products of other and far remote waters, then, with the exception of an occasional settler engaged in clearing up a portion of the wilderness and reducing it to his necessities, or the swiftly gliding canoe of the Indian rippling the placid waters of the streams, all or nearly all partook of the silence of nature.

But leaving the remote past to abler hands, let us come down to a more recent period; there are those present whose recollections take them back to a very different condition of things from what we now see. Even I, at my comparatively early period of life, recollect when New Bedford contained only about three thousand inhabitants; the details of a painting, made some twenty-five years since by one of our native artists, representing the "Old Four Corners," are all familiar to me; many a time have I accompanied my respected father to the shed market there represented; the old store on one of the corners, then and now known as the "Four Corners," with the upper half of the window shutter propped up on a stick, and nearly all the other objects handed down to us of the present day by this picture, I recollect as though they were still extant, not forgetting some of the more prominent persons so faithfully represented, nor yet the little old No. 1 fire engine, nor the old chaise with the small round seat in front, upon which sat old "Tony," when he drove his excellent master, the venerable William Rotch, Sen., through the streets. I have heard my maternal grandmother relate, that when the house which stood upon the north-west corner of Union and First streets, on a portion of the site now occupied by Thornton Block, was raised, she sat at the window of her house on Water street, between School and Walnut streets, and looking *through the forest* witnessed the operation. In that house, many years after I was born, I have been told by an uncle of mine, that when he was a boy, and went with other boys after berries, if they thought to go so far from home as where I now live, on Sixth street, they considered it necessary to take their dinners with them. These, and many other incidents that might be related, show the changes that have taken place in a few years.

I have also very pleasant recollections of many of the old people of forty or more years ago. Of the venerable William Rotch, Sen., before alluded to, who lived in what is now the "Mansion House," who on one occasion, when I was quite a boy, placing his hand upon my head, said to me, "Ah George, I have worn out, I have not rusted out." Of John Howland, my honored grandfather, who was acknowledged by all to have been a strong-minded man, a useful man too, and one who served his generation faithfully, who, once on the evening after a "town meeting" put to me this question: "George, been to town meeting to-day?" I replied, "No, grandfather, why should I go to town meeting?" (being only a boy,) when he immediately added in the style peculiar to that day, "Go to larn." Little did I at that time appreciate the force of the expression, "Go to larn." Whether or not I have heeded the injunction since, I leave for others.

These men, and such as these, acted on the belief that there was something for every one to do, and that it behooved every one to do something. With them there was no place for drones;—would that such sentiments prevailed more fully at the present day. There would be more of "wearing out," and less of "rusting out."

I might name many other noble men of that day, whose descendants are still with us, such as the Allens, the Davises, the Grinnells, the Hathaways, the Rodmans, the Russells, the Spooners, the Tabers, the Thorntons, &c., &c., not omitting some who still live amongst us, and who, by the even tenor of their lives, and the excellent example which they set us, command the admiration and respect of all, and who, I hope, may yet be spared to us for years to come.

When I look over our city, and see the improvements which have taken place within my time, and over the territory represented by you, my fellow-citizens and neighbors, and then go further and embrace our whole country, I sometimes ask myself the question, Can these improvements continue? and will science and art make the same rapid strides for the next fifty or one hundred years, as for the past? The only answer I can make to the query is the real Yankee one; Why not? What reason have we to suppose that we have reached the *ne plus ultra* in anything? Although the steam engine in all its various appliances on the land and on the water, the magnificent clipper ship, the electric telegraph, and the photographic art, are attainments the origin of which is within the recollection of many of us, and which seem, each in itself, to have arrived at a high state of perfection, who of us can say the end has *yet* been reached?

I for one do not think it has; when this wicked rebellion which now presses upon us like an incubus, paralyzing our energies, or forcing us into unwonted channels, shall be ended, and peace shall again smile over our beloved and undivided country, may we not hope to go on improving in all that is real, in all that is enduring, until we shall have reached the highest position to which any country can attain, honorable, dignified, exalted, on a foundation like adamant, with a superstructure of truth and righteousness?

ADDRESS

OF

WILLIAM W. CRAPO.

At a meeting of the committee of arrangements, Sept. 15th, 1864, it was

Voted, That the thanks of the committee be communicated to William W. Crapo, Esq., for his highly interesting, valuable, and appropriate address delivered on the 14th instant, on the day set apart for the commemoration of the two hundredth anniversary of the incorporation of the town of Dartmouth, and that he be requested to furnish the municipal authorities with a copy for the press.

George Howland, Jr., Chairman.

New Bedford, Oct. 1, 1864.

Hon. George Howland, Jr., Chairman, &c.:

My Dear Sir, Yours of the 17th ult., accompanying the vote of the committee on the Centennial Celebration, has been received.

Herewith I inclose to you for publication a copy of the address delivered by me, as requested by your committee.

Yours, very truly,

William W. Crapo.

ADDRESS.

At the June term of the Plymouth Colony court in the year 1664, it was ordered that

"All that tract of land commonly called and known by the name of Acushena, Ponagansett, and Coaksett, is allowed by the courts to be a township, and the inhabitants thereof have liberty to make such orders as may conduce to their common good in town concernments, and that the said town be henceforth called and known by the name of Dartmouth."

This event—the birth of our municipality—demands a recognition.

There are duties which we owe to our fathers as well as to our children. While posterity claims of us a faithful transmission of all the rights and privileges and blessings which have come to us from the past, and insists that we add our contribution to the sum of human progress, our forefathers as justly demand that we recognize by grateful acknowledgments and filial remembrance, their services, self-denial, and heroism. There can be no more fitting occasion wherein to give expression to these sentiments than that which assembles us together to-day, upon the two hundredth anniversary of the municipal existence of the old town of Dartmouth.

The occasion dictates the character of the discourse. The thoughts turn instinctively to the early history of this ancient town, and to the incidents and institutions and men which marked its origin and progress. In no better way can we commemorate the Past than by recalling these events, bringing to memory the names of those who then acted, and reciting their services and deeds. We come together to-day, a family of towns, the children of a common origin, having left from time to time the protection of the old Mother town for that separate corporate existence which the growth of population and the diversity of business interests rendered necessary. We come from all quarters of the old township to celebrate its two hundredth birth-day, reviving the feeling of the family bond by recalling olden times and linking the present with the past. We look back upon this history with the same emotions as those who trace the record of a revered and honored ancestry.

In the year 1664 our town received its corporate existence and name. Let me briefly allude to its history prior to that time. In the summer of 1602 Bartholomew Gosnold, while fortifying his settlement upon the little islet within the island of Cuttyhunk, had crossed the Bay—described by Gabriel Archer, the chronicler of the expedition, as a "stately sound"—and had trod upon our shores. The Indians from the main land had visited him and his band of adventurers in their island home, and Gosnold had returned their visits. He landed somewhere in the vicinity of the Round Hills, called by him Hap's Hill, and followed the coast westward to Gooseberry Neck. The locality is described as possessing "stately groves, flowery meadows, and running brooks," and the adventurers were delighted with the climate, the beauty of the country, and the fertility of the soil.

Gosnold's idea of planting a colony in this vicinity failed, and the territory was uninhabited by the white man until after the landing of the Pilgrims at Plymouth. Looking back over this long period of time we can hardly fail to discern why the settlement at Cuttyhunk was a failure and the settlement at Plymouth a success. Gosnold and Gilbert and Archer and Rosier and Brierton were gentlemen adventurers, in quest of novelty and the excitement of a bold, daring enterprise, with a hope of gain; and when they had unfolded this fair land and had collected a sufficient quantity of sassafras root and cedar and furs to load their little bark, the only bond which then united them was the cargo they had collected, and each one was ambitious to return with it to England to profit by its sale and tell the marvellous stories of their adventures. We do not wonder then that although they found the red and white strawberry "as sweet and much bigger than in England," with "great store of deer and other beasts," and feasted and grew fat upon the young sea fowl which they found in their nests, they did not build up a permanent settlement.

On the other hand, Carver and Bradford and Winslow and Brewster and Standish, the men of the Mayflower, came from far different motives; not from gain, adventure, or novelty, but to plant a colony which should be permanent and enduring; to carry out, heedless of privations and sufferings, heedless of the scorn and oppression behind, and the uncertainties and dangers before, their ideas of a government founded upon equality, justice, and religion. The colony at Plymouth, conquering all obstacles, achieved permanency and growth, and from thence came the early founders of Dartmouth. We are proud of our ancestry,—proud that the men of Dartmouth were Puritans. Those "stout-hearted and God-fearing men" were our fathers. Never can they be mentioned but with honor, for none ever did more or suffered more for the human race. Oppression did not intimidate, nor privations turn them. They were stern and unyielding in their convictions of the right, and thoroughly fixed and resolute in their purpose to found a Christian Commonwealth. Inspired with the one grand idea of a government resting upon liberty and religion, they thought not of policy, expediency, or compromise, but listened only to the dictates of conscience and duty. Under their sturdy and unconquerable wills the wilderness yielded and the new world was opened to a nation of freemen.

In the history of New England not enough prominence has been given to the pioneer colony of Plymouth. The settlement of the Massachusetts Colony seems to have overshadowed in history the importance of this first civil body politic. The Plymouth Colony led the van, and in the years in which they were alone, rested the whole problem. Encouraged by the success of the Plymouth settlement the Massachusetts colonists were emboldened, under the protection and guidance of the former, to apply for a Royal charter. We would not detract from the merit of Winthrop, Dudley, Saltonstall, and their associates, "gentlemen of figure and estate," for they were men of faith and fortitude, men of uncommon wisdom and heroism; but let us not be forgetful of those earlier men who smoothed away some of the rough places of the forest and opened to the men of Massachusetts Bay and Boston, even though for a short distance and in a rude way, the path which led so triumphantly to civil and religious liberty.

On the 29th day of November, 1652, the Indian Chief, Wesamequan (better known as Massasoit,) and his son Wamsutta (who was sometimes called Alexander by the English,) conveyed by deed to William Bradford, Captain Standish, Thomas Southworth, John Winslow, John Cooke, and their associates, all the tract or tracts of land lying three miles eastward from a river called Cushenegg to a certain harbor called Acoaksett to a flat rock on the westward side of the said harbor. In this conveyance was included all the land within these boundaries, "with all the rivers, creeks, meadows, necks and islands that lie in and before the same, and from the sea upward to go so high that the English may not be annoyed by the hunting of the Indians in any sort of their cattle."

The metes and bounds of this grant do not appear to be very definitely or clearly stated. More attention seems to have been given by the conveyancer to the consideration which the Indian chieftains were to receive. The price paid was thirty yards of cloth, eight moose-skins, fifteen axes, fifteen hoes, fifteen pair of breeches, eight blankets, two kettles, one cloak, two pounds in wampan, eight pair stockings, eight pair shoes, one iron pot, and ten shillings in other commodities. Even in those early days, when the forests and meadows and streams apparently were not valued very highly, dissensions and disputes arose concerning the title. A younger son of Wesamequan, Philip, Sagamore of Pokannockett, afterwards known as one of the most bloody and remorseless of all the Indian warriors under the name of King Philip, had not been consulted, or had not given his written assent to the original conveyance. He soon began to annoy the settlers by frequent acts of trespass, and to question the correctness of the boundary lines. We find by the records, that agents—referees—were appointed "to set out and mark the bounds," and in 1665 Philip gave a quit-claim which quieted the title.

This large tract of land, comprising the limits of old Dartmouth, was divided into thirty-four parts or shares. Two of these were subdivided, so that the original proprietors numbered thirty-six persons, of whom three were women—Sarah Brewster, Miss Jennings, and Sarah Warren.

Not all of the thirty-six original proprietors settled here. Some undoubtedly bought the land as a speculation or investment rather than for a home, but an inspection of the names convinces us that many of them located permanently within our borders. We find in the list, the names of Howland, Morton, Manasses Kempton, Dunham, Shaw, Cooke, Soule, Faunce, Sampson, Delano, Bartlett, Palmer, Doty, Hicks, Brown and Bumpass, names familiar to us even in this day, and constantly recurring in the history of the town.

It has always been stated that the old township of Dartmouth included and comprised the present townships of Dartmouth, Westport, New Bedford, Fairhaven, and Acushnet. The grant of land from the Indians embraces these towns. But the records of the colony of Rhode Island show that a part of the present towns of Tiverton and of Little Compton were, prior to 1746, a part of Dartmouth.*

The origin of the name of our town is a matter of conjecture, yet the inference is an easy and natural one. The Mayflower and Speedwell, the latter having taken on board her priceless freight at Leyden in Holland, sailed from Plymouth in Old England, and that name was given to the spot where they landed in New England. After the vessels left Plymouth, England, a disaster occurred to the Speedwell which compelled both vessels to put back, and they made a harbor in the seaport town of Dartmouth in the British Channel. Many of the original purchasers and some of the early settlers of the town came in the Mayflower, and the name of Dartmouth was so associated in their minds with the home left behind that it may naturally be presumed it furnished them with the name for their new home. There is a further coincidence connected with the name. The little vessel — the Concord — which brought Gosnold to our shores in 1602, belonged to Dartmouth, in England. It has been very fairly inferred by one of our local historians that the reports of the fair land they had visited in the new world which were carried back upon the return of this vessel, had been kept alive, and stimulated the adventurous of that seaport town to seek their fortunes here, and give the spot the name of their former home. There can be no doubt but that we derive our name from this fishing town on the river Dart in the English Channel. How wonderful the change since then! While the Dart-

* Records of Colony of Rhode Island and Providence Plantations, vol. 5, p. 204.

mouth whose birthday we celebrate has an aggregate population of thirty-five thousand, with a commerce known over the whole globe, the old town in England, with a population of less than five thousand, is as little known to-day as it was two hundred years ago.

The inquiry naturally suggests itself, What were the prominent causes which led to this settlement ? It might have been due in part to the spirit of emigration and change of locality which displayed itself even in those days as a trait in the New England character; it might have been the rich and fertile soil in the valleys of our rivers, fertile certainly when compared with the sand hills around Plymouth, enticing to agricultural labors ; it might have been the accessible and capacious harbors of the Acushnet and Apponagansett, and the safe and sheltered anchorage they afforded, giving promise of future commercial importance ; and attractions perhaps were found in the winding beauties of the Paskamansett and Acoakset. However much these and kindred influences may have contributed to the early settlement of Dartmouth, there is, in my opinion, a cause beyond them all, and which a careful reading of the records of the colony and the town forces me to adopt as the chief reason for the removal from Plymouth to Dartmouth. I have said our fathers were Puritans. They were more than that — they were the protestants of the Puritans. They were in sympathy with the established government at Plymouth in every thing except the one matter of compulsory taxation for religious purposes. Fully believing in freedom of conscience, they had early conceived a strong aversion to the arbitrary imposition of taxes by the civil power for the support of a ministry with which they were not in unison and over which they had no control. The early records of the town, imperfect and fragmentary as they are, in connection with the history of the colony, plainly tell us how earnestly and even bitterly this controversy was waged, and for how many years it was the source of discord and of persecution. The Plymouth Colony court annually apportioned to the town a tax for the support of ministers, in addition to the Province tax, but the Baptists and Quakers of Dartmouth were inflexible in their resistance to it, and while the province rates were faithfully met, those for the maintenance of ministers were refused. It also troubled our good rulers at Plymouth that our fathers were so negligent in providing stated preaching according to the established puritan faith.

We find this order of the court, passed in 1671:

"In reference unto the town of Dartmouth it is ordered by court, that whereas a neglect the last year of the gathering in of the sum of fifteen pounds according to order of court to be kept in stock towards the support of such as may dispense the word of God unto them, it is again ordered by the court that the sum of fifteen pounds be this year levied to be as a stock for the use aforesaid, to be delivered unto Arthur Hathaway and Sergeant Shaw, to be by them improved as opportunity may present for the ends aforesaid."

But this order, like others, seems to have been of no avail, for three years afterwards, when the inhabitants of Dartmouth had met together for the settling of the bounds of the town, the occasion was seized upon for haranguing the people, "at which time the Governour, Mr. Hinckley, the Treasurer, Mr. Walley, Lieutenant Morton, and John Tomson did engage to give meeting with others to propose and endeavor that some provision may be made for the preaching of the word of God amongst them."

Even the calamity which came upon them at this time from the violence and cruelty of the Indians, in the destruction of their homes and the loss of their property, did not soften the displeasure of the government at Plymouth, but rather served as an opportunity for renewed complaint and upbraiding. This appears by the order of court, passed in October of the following year.

"This Court taking into their serious consideration the tremendous dispensation of God towards the people of Dartmouth, in suffering the barbarous heathen to spoil and destroy most of their habitations, the enemy being greatly advantaged thereunto by their scattered way of living, do therefore order that in the rebuilding and resettling thereof, that they so order it as to live compact together, at least in each village, as they may be in a capacity both to defend themselves from the assault of an enemy, and the better to attend the public worship of God, and ministry of the word of God, whose carelessness to obtain and attend unto we fear may have been a provocation of God thus to chastise their contempt of His gospel, which we earnestly desire the people of that place may seriously consider of, lay to heart, and be humbled for, with a solicitous endeavor after a reformation thereof, by a vigorous putting forth to obtain an able, faithful dispenser of the word of God amongst them, and to encourage him therein ; the neglect whereof this court, as they must and God willing, they will not permit for the future."

However earnestly the Plymouth court were determined to subdue the rebellious and heretical spirit of the early settlers, it does not appear that much success attended the effort. The Quakers and Baptists of Dartmouth were from the same stern, unyielding stock, and they were animated by a sense of religious duty as sincere and exacting as that which influenced the rulers at Plymouth.

Stringent laws were from time to time enacted, but much of the legislation was inoperative, as the people of the town, while complying with the letter of the law, would give no heed to its spirit. Laws were passed in 1692 and 1695 requiring the towns to provide able, learned and orthodox ministers to dispense the word of God. Dartmouth did elect a minister, but the question of orthodoxy then arose. In 1704 the town was indicted for non-compliance with the law. At the town meeting held January 4th, 1705, this indignant reply was sent back to the court:

"To the quarter sessions to be holden at Bristol the 8th day of January, 1705—we understand that our town is presented for want of a minister according to law, to which we answer that we have one qualified as the law directs—an honest man, fearing God, conscientious and a learned, orthodox minister, able to dispense the word and gospel to us."

The name of this minister does not appear upon the records of the town.

In order to meet this question of orthodoxy the Assembly passed a law in 1715, in which the prevention of the growth of atheism, irreligion and profaneness is suggested as a reason of its enactment, in which it was provided that the determination of who should be ministers should rest ultimately with the General Court or Assembly. Dartmouth still refused obedience, and claimed the selection of her own minister. At the March town meeting, 1723, in defiance of an Act of that year, Nathaniel Howland was chosen minister, receiving 55 votes, while Samuel Hunt, a Presbyterian or independent, and the first preacher of that sect in our town, received 12 votes.

The struggle culminated in 1724. In the year 1722 the Assembly of Massachusetts passed an Act to raise one hundred pounds in the town of Dartmouth and seventy-two pounds eleven shillings in the town of Tiverton, (then a part of Massachusetts,) for the support of ministers whose selection was subject to the approval of the General Court. These two towns were the only ones in the Province that had not received any Presbyterian ministers. To blind the eyes of the people this sum was put with the Province tax and was afterwards to be drawn out of the treasury. The spirit with which this was met by the inhabitants of Dartmouth can best be seen by quoting the record of the town meeting held November 26th, 1722. The record says: "It being put to vote whether the whole rate of one hundred eighty-one pounds twelve shillings, called Dartmouth's proportion of our province tax, be made by the selectmen, it passed in the negative. And it was put to vote whether eighty-one pounds twelve shillings, being as we are informed by our Representative, to be our just proportion of our Province tax, be forthwith made by the selectmen of said Dartmouth. Voted that it shall be made. Thirdly, Voted that the charges arising or set on the selectmen of said Dartmouth either by execution on their bodies or estates or in appealing to his Majesty for relief be raised by town rates. Fourthly, Voted that seven hundred pounds be raised on the inhabitants of said Dartmouth by a town rate for securing the selectmen for not making the rate of one hundred pounds, and also for all expenses arising in our sending to England to his Majesty in the above premises. Fifthly, Voted that the selectmen are to be allowed shillings each of them a day for every day they lie in jail on the town account."

The town was thoroughly in earnest. Only five taxpayers protested against this appropriation of the seven hundred pounds. This sum, large for those days, was to be met by the tax of that year, and was not bequeathed to posterity in the form of a town debt. Prior to this — in 1696 — the town had instructed the selectmen not to make the rates sent for by the General Treasurer for this purpose, and in the same year it was voted that Recompence Kirby and Mark Jenne shonld have fifty shillings apiece, part of the money they paid to Captain Pope, upon the account of their being "pressed," — and it was also voted that there should be a rate made of twenty-four pounds for a town fund.

The bold and defiant attitude taken by the town could not be overlooked by the Province Rulers. The refusal of the selectmen to assess the tax was followed by their imprisonment in Bristol jail, where they remained about eighteen months. The persons who were imprisoned were Philip Taber and John Akin, selectmen of Dartmouth, and Joseph Anthony and John Sisson, selectmen of Tiverton, a part of whom were Baptists and a part Quakers. An embassy was sent to England. Thomas Richardson and Richard Partridge, who were Quakers, interceded in their behalf. Their petition, addressed to the King in Council, was an able document, and nobly did it plead for freedom of conscience and security of religion, civil liberty and property. The petition was considered at the Court of St. James on the 2d day of June, 1724, when were present the King's most Excellent Majesty and all the Lords of the privy council, and it was ordered that the obnoxious taxes be remitted, and that Philip Taber and his fellow-sufferers be immediately released from their imprisonment, and the Governor and all other officers of the Province of Massachusetts Bay were notified to yield obedience to these orders.*

This brief but brilliant record of the sacrifices and sufferings, the persistent fidelity and the triumphant success of the humble fathers of the old town of Dartmouth, in the great struggle for the rights of conscience, which is still going on throughout the Christian world, entitles them to a high place in the veneration and gratitude of their posterity. They share, with Roger Williams, the exalted honor of declaring to their rulers, and to the world, that having fled from ecclesiastical oppression in the old world they would resolutely maintain their resistance to it in the new; and that

* Gough's History of the Quakers, vol. 4, p. 219. Benedict's Baptists, vol. 1, pp. 503-4.

through the confiscation of their goods, the incarceration of their persons, amidst all the hardships of a new settlement in the wilderness, and under all the horrors of savage warfare, they would never falter in the assertion and maintenance of the great principle of "perfect liberty in all matters of religious concernment." We, their descendants, have entered into the fruits of these sacrifices and sufferings. Let us never forget to whose heroism and fidelity we owe the priceless blessing of our spiritual freedom,—that it is to the hardy yeomanry who two centuries ago cleared these fields, now waving with the coming harvest, of the primitive forests which covered them, we are indebted as well for "a church without a bishop," as for "a state without a king."

The larger portion of the early settlers were Friends, and we find them recognized as a religious body in the town as early as 1683. Their first meeting house was built in 1699, and was located upon the spot now occupied by them at Apponagansett. Their influence as a sect can be plainly seen and felt even now, and much of the high toned morality, generous and practical philanthropy and pure minded Christianity which have blessed and developed our people is owing to their religious teachings.

Next to the Friends, in numbers and influence, stood the Baptists. John Cooke, whose name we meet with on the first and on nearly every page of the early records of the town as a deputy and a selectman, filling various offices of trust and honor, was a Baptist minister for many years. But this same town official, October 29th, 1670, was fined ten shillings "for breaking the Sabbath by unnecessary travelling thereon." If the record of the case had been preserved it would have appeared, we think, that Elder John Cooke was not a Sabbath-breaker but travelling upon his circuit as a Baptist preacher.

The first Congregational Society was formed at Acushnet. No history of this religious body in our town can be complete without a mention of Samuel West, D. D., who was the pastor of the Congregational Church at Acushnet from 1761 to 1803. Doctor West was a man of great learning, of earnest piety, and sincerely devoted to his pastoral duties. A lover of disputation, he was always ready and keen in argument; possessed of an original and vigorous mind, and thoroughly informed upon all of the doctrinal issues of the day, he was an able champion of the cause he espoused. His memory is cherished not only for his successful labors and his great influence in the religious teachings of a hundred years ago, but for his patriotic services in the war of the revolution. Few men have lived in our town who for so long a period of time exerted so beneficial an influence and commanded so high respect and confidence as Doctor Samuel West.

Nowhere upon the face of the globe has the principle of self government, the capacity and right of men to make laws for themselves and regulate their municipal affairs, been so fully illustrated as in the early history of New England. The most perfect democracies that mankind has ever known are found in the early New England towns. Their town meetings were the places where the whole body of the citizens met, and where were discussed, with equal freedom by every one, all topics of importance, whether local or national, moral or political. Here they learned to understand their rights and privileges as citizens, and acquired moral and intellectual strength to defend them. In those days there was no centralization of official duties and responsibilities as now, the government did not rest upon a few, but every man was compelled to give his time and judgment to the administration of the town affairs. In order to secure that full and prompt attendance upon the deliberations of the town which the business required, Dartmouth voted,—in July 1674—ten years after its organization, "that all town meetings shall begin at 10 o'clock and continue until the Moderator duly release the town, not exceeding four o'clock. Also that all such persons as do neglect for a year all the town meetings shall forfeit to the town six pence apiece, and for coming to the meeting too late three pence an hour."

No wonder that with such rules our early municipal affairs were ably administered. True, some of the legislation of the town may seem to us trivial, for example, that every householder shall kill twelve black-birds between the months of January and May or pay a penalty for the neglect, and that a crow should count for three black-birds, but yet every inhabitant became most thoroughly a part of the town and identified in its prosperity and well being.

This close attention to public business, as might be supposed, was at times annoying and irksome, and efforts were sometimes made by individuals to avoid these duties. In 1751, this article was inserted in the warrant of the annual meeting — "Whereas the Easterly and Westerly villages in said town, experience teaches, have often neglected and omitted their duty in coming to said meetings to help carry on and manage the affairs of said town, especially in the difficult seasons of the year and foul weather, (and not in danger of being chosen to troublesome offices,) and so have at such times trusted and almost entirely relied and depended on the Middle village, of which the body of the people therein inhabiting live remote from said house, to do all the business of said town, which said Middle village is obliged to do though a hardship ; otherwise said town would have incurred many a fine for neglect of duty, the want of grand and petit jurymen, and otherways suffered."

In order to meet this difficulty it was voted to move the town-house. But the removal of the town-house did not remedy the evils complained of, or, if this end was attained new evils arose, for the next year the selectmen inserted an article in the warrant — "To see if the persons who carried away the town-house will bring it back again and set it up in the same place where they took it from, in as good repair as it was when they took it away, and for the town to act on the affair as they should think proper."

This town-house I infer was the one voted in 1739 to be built, the dimensions of which were to be "nine feet between joints and twenty-two feet wide and thirty-six feet long, with a chimney at one end with a suitable roof and windows at the same."

The mode of conducting the town business was similar

to that now adopted, but the style of some of the warrants would not be tolerated in these days. It was customary for the selectmen in calling a town meeting not only to state the business to be considered, but also very elaborately to discuss the several subjects, thereby furnishing to the people not only the question but the arguments in favor of or against it. It might have been that this full presentation of the merits of the case and the reasons for action elicited more attention, and in the language of the old town clerks was productive of "large debate." As an illustration of this peculiar and amusing feature in the presentation of the topics for town action, let me quote from the records.

The sixth article in the selectmen's warrant for the March meeting, 1741, reads thus:

"That whereas such course does much abound within said town, many running about from house to house to supply their own present want miserably neglecting their families at home, which is the only cause of manys suffering who are not capable of labour, which practise is to the grate detriment of that part of the inhabitants that are industrious and laborious, which pernicious practice together with spending idly what they have or earn is a grate if not the only cause of scarcity of bread in said town, now to pass a vote at said meeting for the building a workhouse in said town for the setting and keeping to work all such persons who misspend their time as above stated which said vote is thought by all those that request the same cannot be spoken against except by those which are in danger of breaking into said house themselves."

Another example of this presentation of reasons in the warrant of the selectmen occurs in 1746, when an effort was made to divide the county or create a new county seat. This question both before and after this date engaged the attention of the people of Dartmouth for many years. At one time it was proposed to divide the county and join Tiverton and Little Compton with us as a new county. At another time it was proposed to change the county seat to Assonet as more central than Taunton. The question was finally settled in 1828, after an agitation of over one hundred years, by making New Bedford a half-shire town. The article in the warrant for the town meeting held in 1746 is as follows :

"To consult and vote something with respect to petitioning the General Court that we may have a County taken off or made on this side of Assonet River, otherwise we must unavoidably be expressed to go and our children after us, for what we know, to Taunton, which will be upwards of thirty five miles distance for many of said inhabitants, which will be in the journey extremely tedious and expensive, it being too far to set out from our homes to get there before the Court Setts, as likewise the largeness of the County agravates the case by reason that one case must waite for another and is at times the occasion of adjournment. In the whole it will be tedious and expensive to Plaintiff, Defendant, Jurymen and Evidences. But more especially to Poor Widows who are oft times obliged to go several times before an Estate can be settled with the Judge of Probate."

It was certainly very convenient for the people to

have the arguments all arranged for them before they were called upon to vote. That our fathers took no offence at this course is evident from its constant recurrence.

The topics suggested by an occasion like the present are numerous. The subject is a fruitful one, and there should be written with fullness and accuracy the history of the town. No simple address, however carefully and elaborately prepared, can meet this want. Let this anniversary stimulate and encourage the work. The materials are fast fading away, and in a few years much that can now be recorded with precision and correctness must become a matter of mere conjecture. Of equal, if not of greater importance is the rescue and preservation of our early records, which have been heedlessly and, I am disposed to say, criminally suffered to become lost or destroyed, but whose restoration, so far as possible, is now in able hands.*

In the remaining time allotted to me on this occasion, I can only refer, and that very briefly, to two of the most prominent events of the past two hundred years.

No one epoch of the town deserves to be mentioned more prominently than its devastation by the Indians

* The importance of gathering together and arranging the fragments of town records which are still left to us may be inferred from the action of the town meeting held in May, 1774, when a committee was appointed "to overhaul the town records and make report what part of said records stand in need of new drafting." The committee reported, among other things, that some of the records "were so worn and in pieces and the leaves so defaced that the records stand in danger of being almost wholly lost or obliterated." Although Benjamin Aikin and Benjamin Russell, Jr., were authorized to new draft said records at the expense of the town, yet it does not appear that anything further was done, and there has been ninety years of wear and tear since then with all the casualties of time and neglect.

Measures were taken in 1862, by the authorities of New Bedford and Dartmouth, to have the town records now remaining arranged and copied. James B. Congdon, Esq., was appointed to execute the work, which has been prosecuted with his accustomed earnestness and fidelity and with the most satisfactory progress, ensuring its speedy completion.

during King Philip's war. No other portion of territory was so desolated by the ravages of the savage warfare carried on by this Indian Chieftain. Tradition informs us that every white habitation within the limits of the town was destroyed. The inhabitants took refuge in garrisons — the principal one of which was Russell's garrison, named after John Russell, a prominent man in the town, which was situated near the head waters of the Apponagansett on the east side of the river. Near this on the opposite bank the Indians had a rude fortification. There was also a garrison for the whites on Palmer's Island. During this war Dartmouth was relieved, on account of her home defences, from furnishing any men under the military levies, and during the war and for several years afterwards she was omitted in the tax rates of the colony. It is an interesting fact that while this destitution and suffering existed "contribution was made by divers Christians in Ireland" (so says the record) "for the relief of such as are impoverished, distressed and in necessity by the late Indian war."* How nobly has this charity been returned many times since then by the Christian people of Dartmouth in contributing relief to the famishing and suffering of Ireland! And whenever hereafter the cry shall come from that generous-hearted people for aid and succor, let it be liberally furnished, for it is but the payment of a debt which our fathers have charged upon us.

The other prominent event to which I would allude is the burning of Bedford Village in the war of the

* Plymouth Colony records 1676-7, 6th of March.

revolution. This act of the British army appears to have proceeded from motives of retaliation and punishment rather than for purposes of plunder. Our harbor had from the beginning of the war been noted as a rendezvous for privateers, and the damage inflicted upon English commerce by the whalemen of Dartmouth had excited the deepest resentment. As early as May, 1774—but a few weeks after the skirmish at Lexington and before the battle of Bunker Hill, the British cruiser Falcon had captured in the Bay three vessels belonging to Sandwich. A schooner was fitted out from Dartmouth under the command of Captain Equy which recaptured two of these vessels with fifteen British officers and marines. The captors were perplexed what disposition to make of the prisoners, but they were finally sent to the Provincial Committee of Safety then in session at Cambridge, the headquarters of the American army, and by that body were ordered into confinement at Concord. The privateer Providence, whose name is associated with so many brilliant naval achievements, had her rendezvous here. She was a sloop of about ninety tons, and had formerly been employed in the whale fishery. At one time, it is said, she was under the command of the illustrious John Paul Jones. Her most famous exploit, under Captain Hacker, was with His Majesty's brig Diligent of twelve guns, which she captured and brought into our harbor after a most determined and bloody engagement. The fame of this vessel and other privateers of Dartmouth excited to acts of retaliation and vengeance. Accordingly Major-General Grey, with a fleet of two frigates, an eighteen gun brig, and about thirty-six transports, comprising a force of five thousand men, was ordered to the work of destruction. On Saturday, the 5th day of September, 1778, the British fleet appeared in the Bay. The official reports of the English are well known, but there never has been published any full and detailed American account of this affair. Edward Pope, Esq., a man of distinction and holding a judicial position in the town, furnished a brief notice of it in 1784. I am enabled, from the manuscript collections of a former resident* of the town to present the events of that day as gathered from the lips of those who were actors in its exciting scenes. Perhaps I cannot better use a portion of your time on this occasion than by a recital of those incidents. A company of artillery consisting of about eighty privates had been sent from Boston for the protection of the town. The building occupied by them as barracks was the "Poor House"—a long, low building which stood on Sixth street near the present site of Philip Anthony's dwelling house. The officers quartered at Mrs. Doubleday's, on Water street, a short distance north of the "Four Corners." The company was commanded by Captain James Cushing, Lieutenants Joseph Bell, William Gordon, and James Metcalf. This company, although stationed here, had, a short time previous to the landing of the British, been ordered to Howland's Ferry, now called Stone Bridge. But during the day, Lieutenants Gordon and Metcalf had returned with a small part of the company and one gun. There was a garrison at Fort Phœnix, commanded by Captain Timothy Ingraham, with Lieutenant Foster and thirty-six men,

* Hon. Henry H. Crapo.

where there were eleven pieces of cannon mounted, with a supply of twenty-five casks of powder.

About one o'clock in the afternoon Worth Bates, who lived near McPherson's wharf, at Bellville, and who had been down the Bay fishing, landed at the Fort and informed Captain Ingraham that a British fleet was in the Bay. The fleet soon made its appearance. The two frigates and brig anchored opposite the mouth of the Acushnet River and a little below Clark's Point. A portion of the transports were anchored outside the Great Ledge and opposite the mouth of the Cove, while another portion of them dropped in to the eastward of the larger vessels. The troops, including light horse, artillery, &c., were landed in barges. The larger portion landed on the west side of Clark's Point on the present Alms-House Farm. The others landed on the Fairhaven side a little east of the Fort, behind a point of woods and under cover of the guns of the frigates. The troops which landed on Clark's Point marched up the road now called County street, to the head of Main (now Union) street. At this time it was near sunset. A part of the troops here wheeled to the right, passing down Main street, while the remainder continued their march north on County street. The few men under Lieutenants Gordon and Metcalf (it has been stated there were not fifteen able-bodied men on this side of the river at that time) retreated with their single piece of artillery as the British advanced. At the point now made by the junction of North street with County street, on the west side of County street, were thick woods. Under cover of these woods, William Hayden and Oliver Potter fired upon the troops and killed two horsemen. A few minutes after, three citizens of the town, Abraham Russell, Thomas Cook, aud Diah Trafford, all of whom were armed, were discovered by the British coming up a cross street. When near the corner of County street these three men were fired upon and shot down. Trafford was shot through the heart and died instantly, after which his face was badly cut with the sabres of the British. Cook died about daylight, and Russell about ten o'clock the next morning. Lieutenant Gordon was taken prisoner but afterwards escaped. Lieutenant Metcalf was mortally wounded during the night at Acushnet. He died three days afterwards and was buried with military honors on the hill by the meeting house at Acushnet.

The detachment which marched down Union street immediately commenced the work of destruction. The first buildings fired were the rope-walk and the distillery. Soon after, all the stores and warehouses and a number of dwelling houses and barns were burned, together with every vessel in port except those anchored in the stream. The number of vessels destroyed was seventy, of which four were privateers and eight were large ships laden with valuable cargoes.

Between eight and nine o'clock in the evening the detachment which landed on the east side of the river advanced on the Fort. Two guns were fired at the fleet, and then, after spiking the guns, the garrison retreated to the north and concealed themselves, leaving the colors of the Fort flying. The British supposing the Fort to be still garrisoned, opened a heavy artillery fire upon it, but they soon ceased when no response was made. The enemy discovering the position of the concealed soldiers, fired upon them, wounding a man named Robert Crossman, and taking two prisoners, John Skiff and his father. Before the evacuation of the Fort a train of powder was placed from the magazine to the platform. The British after taking possession applied a slow match to the magazine, which communicated with the train left by the garrison and an explosion occurred sooner than was intended, killing one, if not more, of the British. After burning the barracks, the detachment moved north and effected a junction with the force moving down from Acushnet. The next day the troops re-embarked near the Fort.

The night following, a number of barges came up the river, but were fired upon and driven back, a body of militia at this time having arrived from Middleborough. Major (afterwards General) Israel Fearing displayed great gallantry on this occasion.

On Sunday, the sixth day of September, two tories (named Eldad Tupper and Joseph Castle) who had been driven from the town, instigated the British to send a force into Apponagansett harbor. A family of Akinses, strong whigs, had been chiefly instrumental in the expulsion of the tories, and they were the principal sufferers by this raid. Captain Elihu Akins' dwelling house and a new brig on the stocks, were burned. The dwelling house of James Akins, his brother, and also a house belonging to Meribah Akins, were fired and burned to the ground.

After this the fleet proceeded to Martha's Vineyard, where the enemy seized a large quantity of fire arms, cattle, and sheep, and also one thousand pounds sterling, the latter being a tax recently collected by authority of the Continental Congress.

Dartmouth was in no respect behind her sister towns of Massachusetts in devotion and sacrifice to the cause of liberty. She contributed freely in men and money, and although we find in the military annals of the period no names of distinction belonging to the town, yet we know that her people were thoroughly in sympathy with the revolution. On the nineteenth day of September, 1768, Walter Spooner was appointed by the town to represent it in Faneuil Hall, Boston, to consider what wise and prudent measures should be adopted to prevent the distress and misery which were likely to come upon them by reason of the number of regular troops to be quartered in Massachusetts. In 1774 a town meeting was called "to take into the most mature and serious consideration the melancholy and distressing situation of public affairs of this Province, and to adopt and pursue all those rational and justifiable methods which, by the blessings of Heaven attending our endeavors, will have the greatest tendency to remove from us and our fellow-sufferers those troubles we feel and fear under the present frowns of the British Administration."

The town meeting was held July 18th, 1774. Hon. Walter Spooner, Benjamin Akin, Esq., William Davis, William Tallman, Major Ebenezer Willis, Jireh Willis, Seth Pope, Seth Hathaway, and Hannaniah Cornish, were appointed a committee to prepare and draw up what they should deem most proper as expressing the sense of the meeting, and report in the afternoon for the town's consideration. The report of these gentlemen was accepted. It was Voted—"That we are grieved at being necessitated to act a part which at first view appears unfriendly with respect to our manufacturing brethren and friends in Great Britain and Ireland, but we trust we shall readily be excused by them when they consider that this part of our conduct is wholly designed, and in our judgment will have the greatest tendency of anything in our power, to save both them and us from BONDAGE and SLAVERY, for upon mature consideration we judge the several late unconstitutional acts of the British Parliament have a direct tendency to destroy the harmony which has subsisted among all the British subjects and to entirely abolish the English Constitution and form of government, and therefore as the most probable means to prevent those destructive purposes we unite with our American brethren, and

RESOLVE, That we will not purchase any goods manufactured in Great Britain and Ireland which shall be imported from thence after this day; that we will not purchase any English goods of any hawker or pedler; that we will not purchase any foreign teas whatever; that we will not export any flax-seed to any foreign market; that we do acquiesce in the nature and necessity of raising our proportion of money to pay the Congress and to raise the same by subscription, and that these resolves do remain in force so long as the present grievous acts of the British Parliament remain unrepealed."

At this meeting a committee of correspondence was chosen to act with other committees in America. And also a resolve was passed advancing "the town's proportion of the money to pay the committee of Congress."

In the county Congress held at Taunton the same year "to devise and act on such measures as the exigencies of the times require," the town was ably and patriotically represented.

Not the men alone, but the women of Dartmouth fully entered into the resolutions of non-intercourse with Great Britain. They had their League Society which was more exacting in the observance of its principles than the Ladies' League Associations of the present day. In January 1774, fifty-seven ladies of Bedford Village had a meeting at which they entered into an agreement not to use any more India tea; and having heard that a gentleman there had lately bought some, they requested he would immediately return it. This request he complied with, whereupon the ladies treated him with a glass of "this country wine" and dismissed him, highly pleased with his exemplary conduct. A number of gentlemen present gave him three cheers in approbation of his noble behavior.*

This occurred six months prior to the action of the town meeting, and doubtless contributed much in forming the public sentiment of the town.

There are many other events in our history which deserve a mention. Much might be said upon the circumstances and state of public feeling which attended the separation of the several towns from the Mother town, and the strong local political prejudices and antagonism which existed at times between the different sections of the town. The separation of Fairhaven from New Bed-

* Dodsley's Annual Register, vol. 17, page 97.

ford, the incidents of which are fresh in the minds of many here present, was caused by the earnestness of conflicting political opinions. The same independence of thought and persistency of action which characterized the early settlers in resisting the church-rates, can be seen throughout the whole political history of the town.

Another fruitful theme, and one richly entitled to a place in an address of this nature, is found in the treatment of the negro race by the inhabitants of the town. Dartmouth, and especially New Bedford, for many years has been to them a city of refuge and safety, and here, in a far greater degree than elsewhere, have been held out to these people the encouragements of quiet homes, the benefits of education, and the rewards attending fidelity of labor and diligence in business.

It was in Westport that Paul Cuffee, the negro sailor, merchant and farmer, lived, and they were his determined and manly efforts, and his appeals and arguments, accompanied with a refusal to pay the taxes assessed upon him, on the ground that he had no voice or vote with his neighbors, that finally secured from the Legislature of Massachusetts equal rights of suffrage for the colored man with the white man, — a system which the war of the rebellion is likely to incorporate into the political constitutions of all the States of the Union. Thus we see Dartmouth again in advance of the age, settling within herself another of the great problems in human progress.

Dartmouth, too, has her biographies. Although the peculiar religious training and teaching of her children, through the Society of Friends, has been such that we find few names of distinction in professional or military life, yet no town or city in the world can boast of merchants more truly princely in nobleness of character and far-seeing mercantile ability, or of mechanics more skilled in the arts and craft they practise. William Rotch, Sen., the Christian merchant, and George Claghorn, the builder of the frigate Constitution, are names that any people in any age may cherish with pride.

But time forbids the further mention of these and many kindred topics.

And now, in conclusion, fellow-citizens of Dartmouth, what are the duties and responsibilities attaching to us in view of the Past? We have seen that our fathers were industrious, thoughtful, earnest men; that they were bold and independent in their opinions, resolute and unfaltering in their actions. They call upon us likewise to be brave for the truth, never to yield the right, never to tolerate an unjust enactment or a false public sentiment. Their frugal economy, laborious industry, and temperate, simple habits, enabled them to subdue the wilderness, and secured for them happy and comfortable homes. Their intrepidity and daring upon the ocean, and their energy in business, secured for them wealth and prosperity. The character of our fathers was formed among our granite rocks and sturdy oaks. They were faithful in purpose, patient and persevering in endeavor. They call upon us to resist the temptations of ease, and to stand firm against the encroachments of luxury. They bid us boldly to grapple with the storms of adversity, and with heroic valor and unfaltering faith struggle for the triumphs of human advancement and liberty. Our fathers, who laid so broad the foundations of domestic peace and social order, and established, through much patience and suffering, our glorious institutions, call upon us to exhibit the same piety, integrity and courage in maintaining them. As they prospered, so may we prosper, advancing in resources, intelligence, virtue, and happiness, an enterprising and affluent population, invincible against domestic assaults and foreign violence.

Many of us here present are of the old stock. Let us acquit ourselves as worthy sons of noble sires. Let us emulate their virtues, and meeting the emergencies which arise in our paths practise their self-denial. Thus may we, while mindful of the memory of the great and good who have preceded us — who so faithfully labored for our benefit — receive the homage of grateful commendation from those who years hence will celebrate the return of this anniversary.

POEM.

BY

JAMES B. CONGDON.

At a meeting of the committee of arrangements, September 15th, 1864, it was

Voted, That our thanks are due to James B. Congdon, Esq., for the poem delivered by him on the occasion of the commemoration of the two hundredth anniversary of the incorporation of the town of Dartmouth, and that he be requested to furnish a copy for publication.

George Howland, Jr., Chairman.

His Honor George Howland, Jr., Mayor of New Bedford, Chairman of the committee of arrangements for the Centennial Celebration:

My Dear Friend, The manuscript of the poem read by me on the 14th instant is at the disposal of the committee.

With the highest regard,

James B. Congdon.

New Bedford, September 27th, 1864.

PREFATORY.

Dartmouth was incorporated **1664.** In **1676,** during the war with Philip of Mount Hope every white man's dwelling was destroyed, and the inhabitants who escaped with their lives found refuge in the garrisons. In **1764** the blundering legislation of England began—war soon followed, and in **1778** the raid of General Grey laid the fairest portion of Dartmouth in ruins. The ending of the second century and the beginning of the third finds us again at war. The Indian has not fired our dwellings or massacred our people; no foreign raiders have laid waste our homes or shot down our citizens: but many a home and many a heart between "Cushnet and Coackset" are desolate, and the bones of our strong men and youth are bleaching upon the battle-fields. We celebrate the close of the second century of our municipal existance in the midst of the most awful civil war known in history. A blow is now, as before, aimed at our NATIONAL LIFE; and now, as before, shall we triumph, and secure, may we not hope, liberty for all within our borders and more than a century of peace and prosperity.

POEM.

I.

From *NACATA to † COAKSET'S shore,
Where many a happy home before,
  In peace and plenty stood,
Now silent desolation reigns :
Upon the quiet hills and plains,
Descends full charged with direst woe
The vengeance of the savage foe,
  In storm of fire and blood.

II.

By broad ACUSHNET'S rising shore,
On PASKAMANSET'S banks, no more,
  The peaceful hamlets rest;
By COAKSET'S gently moving stream,
No more the cottage hearth-fires gleam,
No more the happy toilers there
Guide through the soil the cleaving share,
  In healthful labor blest.

* Nacata—generally known as West's Island, belonging to the town of Fairhaven. Many years ago John West gave by will one half of this island to trustees, who were to bestow the income upon the industrious and worthy poor. As but little income was derived from it, the property was sold. The New Bedford monthly meeting of Friends has the appointment of the trustees, and the fund is now a means of relief to many a poor but worthy person.

"From Nacata to Coakset," that is from West's Island to Westport, was the description of the old town of Dartmouth.

† Coakset—Westport. Dartmouth was early divided into three settlements, constantly referred to in the old records. Acushnet, now New Bedford, Ponagansett, the present Dartmouth, and Coakset. The settlements were on the banks of the three rivers generally called by the same names, so that the names sometimes were used for the villages and sometimes for the rivers. The tract of land in the neighborhood of the Acushnet is frequently called the Acushnet country.

III.

Again the kingly *Metacom—
The brave Wampanoag's chief has come
In triumph to his ancient home;
No pale-faced foeman near:
With savage joy his eyes behold
The burning cot, the scattered fold,
The scalp displayed by warrior bold,
The prisoner's torturing fear.

IV.

Thus from the vengeful Philip came
Baptismal rite of blood and flame,
A storm of waste and woe;
Thus by a sad and mournful fate
Were Dartmouth's homes made desolate
Two hundred years ago.

V.

But Pockanocket's king no more
Shall scourge with blood the southern shore;
The gallant Church has met the foe,
And Metacomet's head lies low:
A noble chief in war and chase;
The last of Massasoit's race.
But where is Philip's son?
See holy men in stern debate
Resolve the question of his fate—
The deed of shame is done.

* Metacom, Metacomet, Philip. This warrior is known in our history by all these names. It never has been fully determined what relation he and his brother Alexander bore to Massasoit. By most writers they are called his children, by some his grandchildren, and by others his nephews. Much difference of opinion has been expressed as to his character. Let all who are disposed to judge him harshly remember that he was a monarch struggling for the throne of his ancestors.

All hope forever to destroy,
The mother and her gentle boy
Are sold!! beneath Bermuda's sky,
They toil in life-long slavery.*

VI.

The land had rest — on †CUSHNET'S shore
The red man's whoop is heard no more:
No more on ‡PASKAMANSET'S tide,
The swift canoe is seen to glide:
One hundred years have rolled away,
Since PHILIP with his wild array,
Had fought and fell, and closed the sway
Of Indian Sagamore for aye.

VII.

The land had rest — on hill and plain,
The lights of home are bright again,
And golden fields of ripened grain
  Are waving in the gale:
While by each stream and river's side
The village homes are spreading wide,
And on the peaceful waters glide
  Full many a gallant sail.

* This is a sad but a true story. When the ministers, after the custom in the early days of the Plymouth Colony, were consulted as to the disposition to be made of the widow and son of Philip, they advised that the latter should be put to death. John Hopper, son-in-law of Philip, and Betty Hopper, Philip's grand-daughter, were residents of Rochester and died there. Betty was proud of her descent and refused all intercourse with the common people of her race.

† Acushnet was often written without the A. This letter was added to the names of the three villages — Cushnet, Aponaganset, and Acoakset.

‡ The Slocum's River of the maps. The geographers have connived to get rid of nearly all our beautiful and significant Indian names.

VIII.

On calm ACUSHNET'S western slope,
BEDFORD, the future city's hope,
Is rising in its fortunes bright,
Ambitious that the wood-crowned height
  One day should be its own —
While on the eastern plain we see
Its modest looking vis-a-vis,
FAIRHAVEN, on its quiet way,
To take upon a future day,
  An honored place alone.

IX.

Upon the hill-side's gentle rise,
*"*Between the Rivers*," whence the eyes
Of GOSNOLD saw the sunlight gleam
On field and forest, bay and stream,
  See PADANARAM rest:
Not any lovelier spot, I ween,
Had England's noble captain seen,
Since, by the Virgin Queen's command,
From †DARTMOUTH'S old historic strand,
The wide-spread ocean-field to plough,
He guided forth the CONCORD'S prow
  Upon his venturous quest.

X.

Nor less the prosperous work has sped
At PASKAMANSET'S tidal head:

* The meaning of Padan-Aram.

† Dartmouth, County of Devon, England. See address to the Mayor, Aldermen, and Recorder of Dartmouth, in this publication.

The toiling wheels that clatter there,
The sturdy yeoman's labors share:
With peace and competence are crowned
The humble dwellings ranged around,
  On rocky hill and plain:
A spot to nature's lover dear;*
A spot the poet's heart to cheer:
An honored too — there first appear
The steps of hardy pioneer
  On DARTMOUTH'S wide domain.
Dear to my heart thy rock-ribbed hills,
Thy valleys green, thy gentle rills,
Thy sunny nooks, where 'neath the snows
The fragrant Epigæa blows,
And tempts, ere winter yields her sway,
The blooming maiden's steps away,
In many a wooded, warm recess,
To seek its starry loveliness.

XI.

ACOAKSET, with her sea-washed strand —
† The WEST-PORT of the border land —
The western limit of the sway
And rule of Massachusetts Bay,
  Has sprung to life anew:
Along the gentle ‡ NOQUOCHOKE,
How cheerfully ascends the smoke,

* The scenery in the neighborhood of Russell's Mills, as the village at the head of the tide-waters of the Paskamanset is called, is very attractive. There are many other beautiful spots within the domain of the old town — neither of its divisions being without them. Our fellow-citizen, William Allen Wall, Esq., by a series of paintings in water colors, has, at the same time, exhibited the beauty of our local scenery, and his own rare artistic talent in its delineation.

† "From Eastport to Westport" was the expression that defined the eastern and western coast limits of Massachusetts before Maine became a State.

‡ Westport River.

From cots of sturdy freemen spread,
From *PACHACHUCK to River-Head!
No spot upon the southern shore,
A nobler race of freemen bore:
  To God and country true.

XII.

The patriot's plea was urged in vain;
The dogs of war are loose again.
From o'er the stately †Dartmouth's side
To ruin in the rushing tide,
By patriot hands is hurled the tea,
An offering dear to liberty.
At Bunker Hill and Lexington
Are freedom's battles fought and won.
From Georgia's hot palmetto plain,
North to the pine-clad hills of Maine,
And from the broad Atlantic's shore
To Niagara's thundering roar,
  War's ensigns are unfurled:
War on the mountain and the plain—
War on the river and the main—
War in the crowded city's street—
War in the hamlet's lone retreat;
Wide o'er the groaning land we see
By war's death-dealing enginery,
  The storm of ruin hurled.

XIII.

And who the foeman? whose the hand,
That wields the bloody battle-brand,

* Westport Point.

† The ship Dartmouth, of Bedford in Dartmouth, New England. She was owned by Francis Rotch.

That brings upon the bleeding land
  The storm of war again?
Does a new PHILIP head the strife,
With tomahawk and scalping knife?
Has PONTIAC'S shade returned to life?
  And have the mighty twain,
Summoned from forest, field and flood,
Their warriors to the work of blood?

XIV.

The ranks by Howe and Pigot led,
Which strewed the hill-side with their dead,
And twice in rage and terror fled
  From PRESCOTT'S patriot band—
The foe o'erthrown at Bennington,
Where STARK the double conflict won—
The haughty Burgoyne's boasted power,
At Saratoga brought to cower
  To gallant GATES' command—
The squadrons which in terror yield
At Trenton's glorious battle-field—
The thousands which without a blow,
To WASHINGTON and ROCHAMBEAU,
With grounded arms and colors cased,
Subdued, disheartened and disgraced,
Surrendered! leaving to the free,
Sacred to peace and liberty,
  A consecrated land!—
These are not red men! not the foe
Who came in wide-spread storm of woe,
Summoned a hundred years ago
  From forest, field and flood:

No fierce WAMPANOAG leads the strife;
No OTTAWA grasps the scalping knife,
To end the nation's infant life,
In agony and woe.

XV.

They came from GOSNOLD'S native land—
The birth-place of the PILGRIM BAND—
The mother land of all:
But not like *him*, new worlds t' explore,
Sought they the distant western shore:
And not in Faith' and Freedom's name,
As BRADFORD, STANDISH, WINSLOW came,
At Heaven's appointed call.

XVI.

It was an autumn day serene,
Nature still wore her robes of green;
As summer, bright the sunny gleam
On lake and inlet, bay and stream;
Balmy the quiet western breeze,
That stirred the gently swelling seas,
And rustled through the lofty trees,
On PADANARAM'S height:
On COAKSET'S long and level shore,
Low is the never-ceasing roar;
Beneath *HAPS' double-crested hill,
The gently swelling waves are still;
The GREAT †NAUSHON, the distant ‡NOPE,

* Haps' Hill, thus called by Gosnold, now known as The Round Hills, near the entrance of Buzzard's Bay.

† The largest of the Elizabeth Islands, at one time the favorite residence of James Bowdoin, now owned by John M. Forbes, Esq., of Milton.

‡ Martha's Vineyard.

The sheltered floods of * GOSNOLD'S HOPE,
Clear from the crown of CUSHNET'S slope
  Break sweetly on the sight.

XVII.

Below, the rising † village see
Strong with a vigorous infancy:
From shop and pier and rocky strand,
The music of the craftsman's hand
Is blending with the jovial note
Poured by the tuneful sailor's throat,
From many a gallant craft afloat
  On calm ACUSHNET'S tide.
Beside the rude unfinished quay,
The modest looking whalers lay;
While swinging at her moorings near
Is seen the jaunty privateer;
Tall ships with flag and pennon gay,
Bright flashing in the sunny ray,
With many a gentle sail between,
Give life and gladness to the scene
  Of beauty and of pride.
Yet ere this western sun shall set
Beyond the woods of ‡ SECONET,
The gazer from ACUSHNET HEIGHT
Shall look upon far other sight—
Shall see approaching from afar,
"The pomp and circumstance of war."

* Buzzard's Bay. Gosnold fared much like Columbus. But few of the names given by him have been retained.

† Bedford.

‡ Seconet Point, the southern extremity of the town of Little Compton, R. I., the town bordering on Westport.

And ere the moon the coming night,
Shall yield to day her waning light;
The gazer from ACUSHNET HEIGHT
Shall look with horror and affright
  On ruin deep and wide.

XVIII.

Why on *POINT PERIL'S reach of sand,
Inactive does the fowler stand?
Why heeds he not the feathered prey
Which near him wing their southern way?
Why is his fixed and troubled eye
Intent upon the western sky?
"THEY COME!" he cries — at once he knew
The hardy boatman's story true:
That he had seen for many a day,
A vast and terrible array
Of ships whose crowded decks betrayed
The secret of the coming raid,
With mighty war-craft riding near,
Along whose lofty sides appear
The guns which thunder forth the power
Of Britain in the conflict's hour.

XIX.

"They come!" exclaims the fisher-boy,
Among the rocks of †BARNEY'S JOY —
And from the heights of bald †MISHAUM,
The farmer sees the threatening storm:

* Gooseberry Neck of the maps, in Westport, near Horse Neck. Upon the latter is that beautiful beach, the rival of Nahant. This is a noted place for the sportsman. The sea-fowl in their annual migration fly across this sandy beach, and great numbers are taken.

† Points of land projecting from the southern shore of Dartmouth.

"They come!" he cries, "they come!"
And quickly from HAPS' lofty hill
Starts forth the messenger of ill,
And through the forest pathway hies
To where in peace ACUSHNET lies,
And shouting as he leaps, he cries,
"They come! they come! they come!"

XX.

Majestic moves the vast array,
Nor pauses on its eastern way —
And now from PONAGANSETT'S height,
The village group have caught the sight,
As bending in the gentle gale,
With streamers gay and sun-lit sail,
The leader's prow directs the way,
O'er the smooth surface of the bay,
To where ACUSHNET'S waters lay
In evening's calm repose.
The * Carysfort is on the van —
Secure with traitor † guide she ran;
Her consorts' guns protect the rear,
While lofty ships between appear
In crescent line, whose work of fear
Their swarming decks disclose.

XXI.

A gun! from ‡ WINSEGANSETT shore
Returns the startling echo's roar:

* See the address of Mr. Crapo in this publication.

†. The fleet had a tory pilot from Padanaram.

‡ A part of Sconticut Neck, the southern extremity of Fairhaven, forming the eastern shore of the lower part of the Acushnet.

Each ship th' appointed signal hears,
And quickly to the windward veers;
With sails aback, like generous steed
Checked in his swift and graceful speed,
The convoy in its proud array
Rests on the bosom of the bay.
It is the boatswain's whistle shrill
That darts along the waters still;
The ponderous anchor loosened now,
Drops from each vessel's stately prow;
With magic speed and hearty cheers,
The furling canvas disappears;
Ranged by the transports' lofty side
The boats are resting on the tide.
Wide o'er the quiet waters float
The sound of drum and bugle's note:
The boats below in order wait;
And quickly with a warrior freight,
Each to the gunwale laden deep,
They onward to * CLARK'S headland sweep.

XXII.

Ne'er had yon island-belted bay
Beheld so gallant an array:
No foe so mighty e'er before
Had landed on New England's shore.
The ships are swinging to the tide;
While o'er the parting waters glide
Long lines of boats, by bending oar
Moved quickly to the fated shore.
The glassy surface of the bay

* Clark's Point, the southern extremity of New Bedford, running out into Buzzards Bay.

Reflects the hues of parting day;
Each red-clad warrior's burnished gun
Is flashing in the setting sun,
Which brightens with its closing ray,
Saint George's meteor standard gay,
Drooping in graceful lines of red,
From mizzen-peak and topmast-head.
The stately barge that proudly bore
The lordly chief, has reached the shore:
And ere the gently fading light
Had yielded to the reign of night,
Ranged on that woody headland's strand,
Four thousand veteran warriors stand.

XXIII.

Now moving to their destined prey,
The close-formed ranks are on their way,
And soon they reach the gentle rise,
Whence to the east the village lies.
A halt — and does the veteran * Grey,
The work of spoil and vengeance stay?
Say, does he at this lovely hour,
Brief homage pay to beauty's power,
And pause ere to the spoiler's hand
He gives the desolating brand,
To change a scene so sweet and fair,
To wide-spread ruin and despair.

XXIV.

The full-orbed moon a flood of light
Pours on the bosom of the night;

* There was but little romance about General Grey. He was a Peer of England and father of Lord Grey of Reform Bill notoriety.

The quiet waters of the bay
Are burnished by the gentle ray,
And calmly on its silvered breast,
The foeman's ships at anchor rest.
Below the broad ACUSHNET'S stream
Is brightened by the silvery beam,
Which to the vengeful raider's gaze
The thickly crowded fleet displays—
The treasure-bearing ships that ride
At rest upon the gentle tide.
At hand beneath the gazer's eye,
The dwellings of the village lie;
And ranged along the rocky strand,
Full many a shop and warehouse stand,
Each on that calm and lovely night,
Seen clearly in the flooding light.

XXV.

And who is he, with gentle mien,
Now gazing on this lovely scene?
Apart he stands, and with delight
Drinks in the beauty of the night.
As in that calm and peaceful hour,
He owns the sway of beauty's power,
The wood, the village, and the stream,
With England's loveliest features gleam;
With soul to love and beauty true,
He sees clear rising on his view,
That British home, that cherished spot,
The home of her, who o'er his lot
Has spread the shade of doom.

He thinks not of the war, the raid;
His heart is with HONORA SNEYD:
And as her features sweet and fair
Crown every thought and feeling there,
He, from its secret resting place
Draws the dear image of her face,
And by the moon-beam's welcome light,
With rapture views those features bright
  With beauty's richest bloom.
In that adoring soldier see
The flower of British chivalry.
ANDRE!—the beautiful and brave!
So soon to fill a felon's grave.
No shadow of a coming woe
Darkens the tender moment's glow;
No vision sad is imaged there
Of treason, capture, and despair.
ANDRE! how dark that hour had been,
Hadst thou that awful future seen!—
The patriots stern who speak thy doom—
The fettered limb, the dungeon's gloom—
  *The gibbet, and the tomb.

XXVI.

"Forward!"—and now the war's array
Is moving on its northern way.
A flash, a sharp report, a groan—
The mighty column passes on.

* There can be no doubt of the fact of Andre's participation in the raid upon Bedford under General Grey. See the official accounts in "The Remembrancer or Impartial Repository of Public Events," 7th vol. p. 36, and Sargent's "Life and Career of Major John Andre," page 194. For the incident of the picture see "Irving's Life of Washington," volume 4th, page 109.

The neighbors by the morning light,
Shall look upon a ghastly sight—
Shall by the crimsoned road-side spy
The Dartmouth dead and dying lie:
Moved to a friendly shelter near,
The flickering life shall disappear,
And side by side in death are laid
These victims of the British raid.
And ere that raiding host has sped
Across ACUSHNET'S tidal-head,
Another volley ringing clear,
The scattered villagers shall hear:
True to its mark the missile flies,
And gallant *METCALF bleeding lies.
His country's martial garb he wore;
His country's loved commission bore:
To-morrow o'er his honored grave
His country's shrouded flag shall wave,
And thrice the volleyed peal shall tell
That METCALF for his country fell.

XXVII.

The river crossed, the war's array
March southward on their weary way;
And ere the coming morning's light
Shall lift the curtain of the night,
Near where their ships at anchor ride,
Upon the peaceful river's tide,
Shall bivouac by th' ACUSHNET'S side.

† See Mr. Crapo's address.

XXVIII.

And was the work of vengeance o'er
Upon th' ACUSHNET'S moon-lit shore?
Had Grey his master's bidding done
When such a field as this was won—
When RUSSELL, COOK, and TRAFFORD died,
And from the gallant METCALF'S side,
Was gushing forth the crimson tide?
From whence the wild demoniac cries
Which from the fated village rise?
From whence that wide and spreading light
That bursts upon the startled sight?
What means that loud, unceasing roar,
That rolls along th' ACUSHNET'S shore?
See by the flame's revealing glare,
A band of British raiders there:
Crazed by the demon of the * still,
They work their vengeful master's will.
Like furies fierce, in either hand
They bear aloft the burning brand,
And speed the midnight work of shame,
By spreading wide the raging flame.
See them from store to store-house go,
And blazing brands around them throw;
Nor do they in their fury spare,
The humble village dwellings there.
Not METACOMET'S Indian band,
When, at their sagamore's command,
Descending in an awful flood
Of desolating flame and blood,

* The distillery was one of the first buildings destroyed, and the excesses of the soldiers were, no doubt, to a great extent, owing to the contents of the vats.

A hundred years before,
They shouted in their savage glee,
The white-man's burning home to see,
The tortured prisoner's agony,
And murdered victim's gore,
With deeper hate or fiercer joy,
Went to their demon-like employ.

XXIX.

And now a flood of flame and smoke
Wide o'er the fated village broke.
Hope, home and dear-bought wealth expire
Wrapped in a winding sheet of fire!
The river's placid breast below
Reflects the fiery column's glow,
Revealing in its horrid glare
The treasure-laden vessels there.
Quickly the frenzied raiding crew,
The helpless, floating, prey pursue.
The flames upon the river's side,
At once a ready torch supplied;
And while from burning village site,
Undimmed, the arch of lurid light
Illumes the bosom of the night,
Forth from the crowded fleet there came
Another pyramid of flame,
Joining its awful light and roar,
To fiery column from the shore.
And now towards the reddened sky,
The mingled flames are mounting high,
And with the brightest glare of day,
Spreading o'er river, hill and bay;

And with a telegraphic glare,
Shall wide the tidings sad declare,
That by the British foeman's raid,
ACUSHNET is in ruin laid —
That on OLD DARTMOUTH'S wide domain
The storm of war has burst again —
And that in blood and flame and tears
Has closed the century of years.

XXX.

One hundred years have rolled away
Since England, in a luckless day,
Strove to enforce a tyrant's sway
  Upon this western world;
And near a century of years,
On history's sealed page appears,
Since by the haughty Briton's hand
Fierce on our firm united land
  The bolts of war were hurled —
Again by sad and mournful fate,
Fair Dartmouth's homes made desolate.

XXXI.

What means that weeping widow's wail,
And what that sorrowing orphan's tale?
Why flow that mourning mother's tears?
And whence that father's brooding fears?
And why with every passing hour,
Flashed by the swift-winged lightning's power,
Come tidings from the field and flood,
Of rapine, ruin, and of blood?

XXXII.

The dogs of war are loose again—
War on the mountain and the plain—
War on the river and the main—
War in the crowded city's street—
War in the hamlet's lone retreat—
Wide o'er the land the work we see
Of war's death-dealing enginery.

XXXIII.

You crave not of the muse to-day
The story of the mighty fray:
Small need have I the tale to tell,
Why *RANDALL fought, why †RODMAN fell.
It was a fratricidal blow
That laid our noble townsman low—
A brother's and a traitor's hand
That crushed the glorious Cumberland!

* William Pritchard Randall, of New Bedford.

"We reached the deck. There Randall stood:
'Another turn, men,—so!'
Calmly he aimed his pivot gun:
'Now, Tenny, let her go!'

"Brave Randall leaped upon the gun,
And waved his cap in sport;
'Well done! well aimed! I saw that shell
Go through an open port.'

"It was our last, our deadliest shot;
The deck was overflown;
The poor ship staggered, lurched to port,
And gave a living groan.

"On board the Cumberland, March 8, 1862." By GEORGE H. BOKER.

† Lieutenant Colonel William Logan Rodman, of New Bedford, killed at Port Hudson, May 27th, 1863. He was attached to the 38th regiment. New Bedford paid a large part of her debt to the country when she sent Colonel Rodman to the battle fields of freedom. But he stands not alone. Of "living valor in the field," and of "valor sunk to rest," New Bedford, and the towns which, with her, once formed the territory of Old Dartmouth, can display a roll at which their children will not need to be ashamed when the muse of history shall make the enduring record.

XXXIV.

Hail! to our Chiefs on sea and land—
All honor to the warrior band,
Who firm a living bulwark stand:
  Green be the soldier's bays;
To living valor in the field,
To valor sunk to rest, we yield
  Our gratitude and praise.

www.ingramcontent.com/pod-product-compliance
Lightning Source LLC
LaVergne TN
LVHW021417110826
845150LV00007B/1960

* 9 7 8 1 4 2 5 5 1 0 2 3 7 *